dressing up
18" DOLLY™

Designs by Lorine Mason

HOUSE of
WHITE
BIRCHES

PUBLISHERS
SINCE 1947

2

Table of Contents

*Floral Drop-Waist Dress, **page 16***

*Asian-Inspired Pajamas, **page 36***

*Glitzy Holiday Dress, **page 8***

*Wrap Dress, **page 13***

*Wool Dress Coat, **page 33***

Dressing Up 18" Dolly

I am so pleased to offer another look at doll-clothing designs using fabric fat quarters. The first book opened the door to designing and writing the next chapter: *Dressing Up 18" Dolly* in cool-weather fashions.

Fat quarters are genius, frankly, and fabric stores, whether online or storefront—my personal favorite—have found that pre-cutting and creating coordinating arrangements of brightly colored fabric swatches attracts customers. Like lollipops in the candy-store window, these displays start the creative juices flowing in their customers' minds. Add to that the price point and ease of buying, and you have a winning combination for both the consumer and the retailer.

When deciding what kind of clothes I should feature in this book, I found myself scanning the advertisements in my Saturday newspaper looking for ideas. I wanted to mix in some contemporary fashion looks through design, pattern and color choices. You will notice this in the shape of the collar on the coat design, the gathering above the knee of a pant-leg design and the color blocking of the A-line dress. At times, I just knew when I picked up a fat quarter what it was meant to be. The shirtdress fabric is a perfect example. It is not a print I would usually be drawn to, but as soon as I spotted it, I had to have it. That's the joy of making doll clothes from fat quarters—utilizing fabrics not normally found in your stash.

My hope is that you have as much fun creating clothes for your 18-inch doll as I did in selecting the fabrics, designing the outfits and writing this book.

Sew far sew good,

Lorine Mason

Meet the Designer

Lorine Mason is an author, project designer and regular columnist whose work has been featured in print, on the Web and television. She works with a variety of art mediums, combining them with her enthusiasm for all things fabric. She strives to create items others will be inspired to re-create, hopefully adding their own personal touches. Her creative career started in retail, weaving its way through management and education. This experience, along with a goal to stay on top of trends in color and style, gives her current work the edge manufacturers, publishers and editors have come to expect. She shares her life with husband, Bill, and daughters, Jocelyn and Kimberly, in Virginia.

House of White Birches, Berne, Indiana 46711   Clotilde.com

General Instructions

The Fit Factor

Using a generic term such as 18-inch dolls can be misleading since dolls, not unlike people, will not have the same measurements even if their height might be similar. A few minutes spent measuring your doll is a good idea. When drafting the patterns for this book, I used 11 inches for the chest and waist measurements, and 12 inches for the hip measurement.

The clothing designs featured in this book were fitted using the Springfield Collection® and the American Girl® 18-inch dolls. I found the American Girl dolls were slightly larger, therefore I took this into account when drafting the patterns. I know there are many other varieties of dolls for which you might be inclined to use these patterns, therefore take a moment and measure your dolls before proceeding, being sure to make any necessary pattern adjustments before cutting out your pattern pieces.

Fabric Selection

All of the outfits and accessories in this book were made using fat quarters. Available in colorful patterns and packaging, fat quarters are the "candy" in the fabric store and are a wonderful way to coordinate fabrics. Generally available in 18 x 22-inch cuts, fat quarters are equivalent to standard 9 x 45-inch quarter yards, and any cotton fabric is suitable for these patterns.

Basic Sewing Supplies & Equipment
- Sewing machine and matching thread
- Scissors of various sizes, including pinking shears
- Rotary cutter(s), mats and straightedges
- Pattern-tracing paper or cloth
- Pressing tools such as sleeve rolls and June Tailor® boards
- Pressing equipment, including ironing board and iron; press cloths
- Straight pins and pincushion
- Measuring tools
- Marking pens (either air- or water-soluble) or tailor's chalk
- Seam sealant
- Hand-sewing needles and thimble
- Point turners

Optional Supplies
- ¼-inch-wide double-sided basting tape
- Hook-and-loop tape
- Bias tape maker
- Tube-turning tool
- Mini iron
- Serger

Construction & Application Techniques

Bobbins
Fill multiple bobbins ahead of time with neutral colors of thread. A cream-colored thread was used for many of the garments in this book. Change only the top color of thread to either match or contrast with garment colors.

Basting
Basting is a way to hold fabric pieces in place without using pins. It is especially useful in tight places or on small projects. Basting can be done by hand or machine using a longer-than-normal stitch length to sew where indicated. Remove basting stitches after garment is permanently sewn.

Backstitching
Backstitching at least ¼ inch at the beginning and end of each seam to secure stitching. This ensures handling does not undo your seams.

Finishing Raw Edges
Every exposed seam should be finished for longer wear and cleaner construction. Finish raw edges with zigzag or overcast stitches or by using a serger. This can be done to each garment piece prior to sewing the garment or during construction.

Gathering
1. Make two rows of longer-than-normal stitches on either side of the seam line, leaving long thread tails at either end (Figure 1).

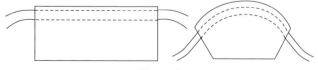

Figure 1

2. With right sides together, pin gathered section to appropriate garment section at each end and at the center (Figure 2).

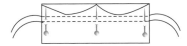

Figure 2

3. Pull bobbin threads at one end to gather. When half of gathered section fits straight-edge length, secure bobbin threads by twisting around pin (Figure 3). Repeat for second half of section. Pin securely along seam line, adjusting gathers evenly.

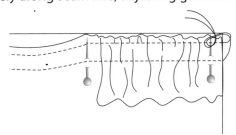

Figure 3

4. Stitch at seam line with gathered section on top (Figure 4). Keep gathers even so folds of fabric do not form while stitching.

Figure 4

5. Remove gathering stitches after sewing seam.

Topstitching

Topstitching provides a decorative touch, while strengthening seams and edges. Because of the ¼-inch seams used in these projects, we suggest topstitching open seams from the wrong side. Stitch approximately ⅛ inch from the seam line or from the finished edge.

Bias-Tape Bound Edges

1. Leaving bias tape folded, sandwich raw edges of garment between bias tape so the fabric raw edge meets the center fold of the bias tape (Figure 5).

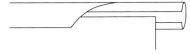

Figure 5

2. Edgestitch bias tape to secure (Figure 6). *Note: Purchased bias tape has one side wider than the other. Be sure to edgestitch with shorter side up when using purchased bias tape.*

Figure 6

Bias-Tape Hems & Casings

1. Press center fold of bias tape flat, leaving edges folded (Figure 7).

Figure 7

2. Pin raw edge of bias tape along fabric raw edge and stitch in edge fold (Figure 8).

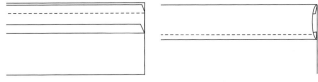

Figure 8   **Figure 9**

3. Press bias tape to wrong side and stitch along edge fold (Figure 9).

Collars

1. Mark collar neckline center. Pin and stitch collar sections right sides together using a ¼-inch seam allowance. Do not stitch neckline seam (Figure 10).

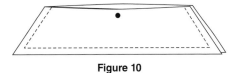

Figure 10

2. Carefully clip curves on rounded collars, and trim points on pointed collars (Figure 11). Turn, using point turner in corners. Press.

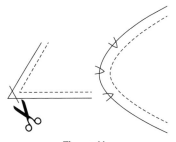

Figure 11

House of White Birches, Berne, Indiana 46711   Clotilde.com

3. Pin, and then baste collar to garment neckline, matching collar center to garment center back (Figure 12).

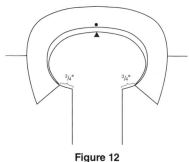

Figure 12

4. Collar will be stitched in place when facing is applied.

Facings

1. Stitch facings together at center back seam (Figure 13). Press seam open.

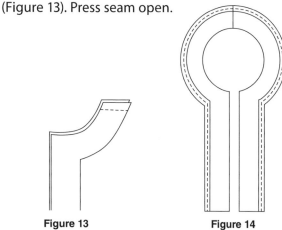

Figure 13   **Figure 14**

2. Apply bias tape to outside edges (Figure 14). *Note: Refer to General Instructions on bias-tape application for bound edges.*

3. Pin facing to garment neckline and front edges, right sides together. Stitch using ¼-inch seam allowance (Figure 15).

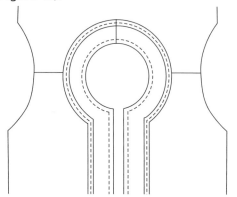

Figure 15

4. Clip curves and trim corners (Figure 16). Turn to right side and press.

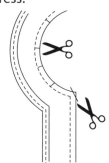

Figure 16

5. Edgestitch facing through all layers using coordinating thread (Figure 17).

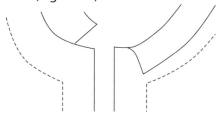

Figure 17

Sleeves

1. Stitch two rows of gathering stitches at sleeve cap (Figure 18). *Note: Refer to General Instructions on gathering (page 4).*

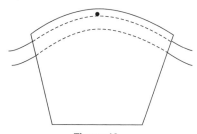

Figure 18

2. With right sides together, pin sleeve cap center to garment shoulder seam and edges of sleeve to garment sides (Figure 19). Gather sleeve cap to fit garment armhole and pin securely.

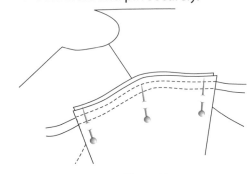

Figure 19

3. Stitch using a ¼-inch seam allowance. Press seam allowance toward sleeve (Figure 20).

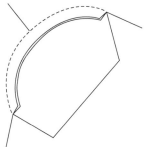

Figure 20

4. With right sides together, match armhole seams and pin underarm seam. Stitch using a ¼-inch seam allowance (Figure 21).

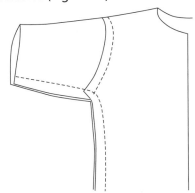

Figure 21

Single Hem
1. Press at least ¼ inch to wrong side of garment (Figure 22).

Figure 22

2. Measuring from the folded edge just made, press the hem width indicated in individual instructions to garment wrong side (Figure 23).

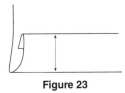

Figure 23

3. Edgestitch close to second fold (Figure 24).

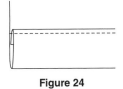

Figure 24

4. If desired, use a contrasting thread to add a simple decorative finish to hems.

Double-Turned ¼-Inch Hem
1. Press ¼ inch to wrong side of section (Figure 25).

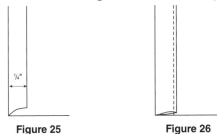

Figure 25   **Figure 26**

2. Turn and press again ¼ inch to wrong side. Edgestitch close to second fold (Figure 26).

Fastener Application
1. Try finished garment on doll to determine where fasteners should be positioned to fit doll's girth.

2. Mark position with pin, lapping garment right side over left (Figure 27).

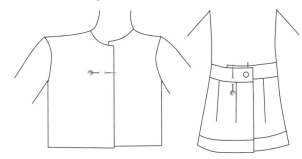

Figure 27

3. Apply ½-inch pieces of fusible hook-and-loop tape to right and left sides of garment where marked. Add decorative closures to right side of garment over hook-and-loop tape.

Option: If using snaps, sew male side of snap to right side, and female side of snap to left side of garment (Figure 28). ❖

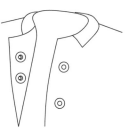

Figure 28

Glitzy Holiday Dress

Materials
- 1 holiday-print fat quarter
- 1 yard coordinating marabou trim
- 1 package coordinating ½-inch-wide single-fold bias tape
- 1 yard coordinating sheer ¾-inch-wide ribbon
- 6 small hot-fix crystals
- 2 (4-inch) lengths ¼-inch-wide elastic
- 1½ inches ¾-inch-wide heat-activated fusible hook-and-loop tape
- Basic sewing supplies and equipment

Cutting
Use pattern templates CC, DD and EE (page 42). Transfer all pattern markings to fabric.

From fat quarter:
- Cut one bodice front (CC) on fold.
- Cut two bodice back (DD), reverse one.
- Cut two sleeve (EE), reverse one.
- Cut two 6 x 16-inch strips for skirt.

From ¾-inch-wide heat-activated fusible hook-and-loop tape:
- Cut three ½-inch fasteners.

Assembly
Stitch right sides together using a ¼-inch seam unless otherwise specified. Refer to General Instructions (page 4) for finishing all seams, and for the following construction techniques: Bias-Tape Bound Edges, Sleeves, Gathering, Double-Turned ¼-inch Hem, Fastener Application.

1. Stitch bodice front (CC) to bodice backs (DD) at shoulder seams.

2. Stitch bias tape to neckline of bodice. Turn tape to wrong side, leaving bias tape showing above neckline (Figure 1). Stitch two rows topstitching around neckline, again referring to Figure 1.

Figure 1

3. Bind bottom edges of sleeves using bias tape.

4. Using a narrow zigzag stitch, sew elastic to sleeve where indicated, stretching elastic to fit. Stitch sleeves to bodice.

5. Stitch two 6 x 16-inch skirt strips together along one short side. Press seam to one side. On right side, position pins 1 inch on either side of seam (Figure 2). Fold fabric so that the pins meet at seam, creating a center front pleat, again referring to Figure 2. Press and baste to secure.

Figure 2

6. Gather and stitch skirt to bodice, centering skirt pleat at bodice center front.

7. Pin ribbon to right side of bodice at waistline (Figure 3). Stitch both edges of ribbon to bodice.

Figure 3

8. Stitch a double-turned ¼-inch hem along back edges of dress.

9. Turn and press ¼ inch to right side of skirt hem edge, and stitch. Hand-stitch marabou trim over hem edge.

10. Apply hot-fix rhinestones to center front of bodice following manufacturer's instructions.

11. Apply three fusible hook-and-loop tape fasteners to back of dress.

12. Tie a bow with remaining ribbon and stitch to center front of dress over ribbon at waistline to complete dress. ❖

Tunic & Pants

Materials
- 3 coordinating fat quarters (A, B, C)
- 11 inches ¼-inch-wide elastic
- 1½ inches ¾-inch-wide heat-activated fusible hook-and-loop tape
- 3 (½-inch) buttons
- Basic sewing supplies and equipment

Cutting
Use pattern templates H, I, J, K, L, M and N (pages 41, 43-46), following cutting lines for Tunic and Pants on multiple-garment patterns. Transfer all pattern markings to fabric.

From Fat Quarter A:
- Cut two tunic fronts (J), reverse one.
- Cut one tunic back (K) on fold.
- Cut two sleeves (L), reverse one.
- Cut one 2 x 22-inch strip for belt.

From Fat Quarter B:
- Cut two collars (M) on fold.
- Cut two facings (N), reverse one.

From Fat Quarter C:
- Cut two pants fronts (H), reverse one.
- Cut two pants backs (I), reverse one.

From ¾-inch-wide heat-activated fusible hook-and-loop tape:
- Cut three ½ x ¾-inch fasteners.

Assembly
Stitch right sides together using a ¼-inch seam unless otherwise specified. Refer to General Instructions (page 4) for finishing all seams, and for the following construction techniques: Topstitching, Collars, Facings, Bias-Tape Hems & Casings, Fastener Applications and Double-Turned ¼-Inch Hem.

Tunic
1. Folding right sides of tunic back (K) together, sew along tuck-stitching line at center back from neckline to X. Press tuck to one side. Topstitch from neckline down stitching line and across tuck to X (Figure 1).

Figure 1

2. Sew fronts (J) and back (K) together at shoulder seams. Press seams open.

3. Construct and stitch collar (M) to tunic neckline.

4. Construct and stitch facings (N) to tunic.

5. Apply bias tape to tunic body and sleeve hems.

6. Stitch sleeves (L) to tunic.

7. Fold 2 x 22-inch strip for belt in half, right sides together, and stitch lengthwise edge. Center seam on one side and press. Turn right sides out. Tuck ¼ inch to inside on short ends; press and pin to hold. Topstitch belt around all edges.

8. Mark center of belt length. Position belt center on tunic approximately 3½ inches from neckline at center back seam. Topstitch belt onto tunic (Figure 2).

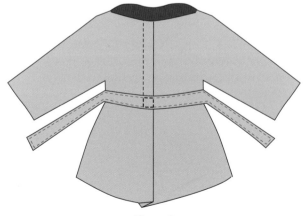

Figure 2

9. Apply three fusible hook-and-loop tape fasteners to front opening. Position the first fastener approximately 2½ inches from the neckline and space 1 inch apart, centered on facing area.

10. Sew three ½-inch decorative buttons to the right side of the tunic front at the hook-and-loop tape positions.

Tunic Pants

1. Fold and press wrong sides together along center front fold line on each pant front (H) piece. Stitch close to pressed fold to form pin tuck (Figure 3).

Figure 3

2. Stitch pant fronts (H) to pant backs (I) along side seams (Figure 4). Press seams toward back. Topstitch in place.

Figure 4

3. Stitch center front pants seam, referring to Figure 5. Press seam to one side and topstitch in place.

Figure 5

4. Create an elastic casing by turning ⅛ inch to wrong side along waistline. Press. Turn to wrong side again along casing line. Press and pin along first fold to hole. Stitch close to first fold line (Figure 6).

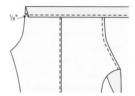

Figure 6

5. Thread elastic through casing. Pin ends of elastic even with back seams of pants and stitch to secure (Figure 7).

Figure 7

6. Stitch a double-turned ¼-inch hem to bottom of each pant leg.

7. Stitch pants center back seam. Press to one side and topstitch in place. Sew inner leg seams to complete pants. ❖

Wrap Dress

Materials

- 2 identical fat quarters
- 1 package coordinating ½-inch-wide single-fold bias tape
- 1 package coordinating ½-inch-wide double-fold bias tape
- 1½ inches ¾-inch-wide heat-activated fusible hook-and-loop tape
- 8 (¼- to ⅜-inch) buttons
- General-purpose thread to contrast with bias tape
- Basic sewing supplies and equipment

Cutting

Use pattern templates L, T, U, V and W (pages 41, 47-49), following cutting lines for Wrap Dress on multiple-garment patterns. Transfer all pattern markings to fabric.

From matching fat quarters:

- Cut two bodice fronts (T), reverse one.
- Cut one bodice back (U) on fold.
- Cut two sleeves (L), reverse one.
- Cut two skirt front (V), reverse one.
- Cut two skirt back (W), reverse one.
- Cut one 2 x 22-inch strip for belt.

Assembly

Stitch right sides together using a ¼-inch seam unless otherwise specified. Refer to General Instructions (page 4) for finishing all seams, and for the following construction techniques: Backstitching, Bias-Tape Bound Edges, Topstitching, Sleeves, Double-Turned ¼-Inch Hem, Bias-Tape Hems & Casings, Fastener Application.

1. On bodice back (U), fold tucks by matching line A to line B, right sides together. Stitch along lines from bodice waistline to X (Figure 1).

Figure 1

House of White Birches, Berne, Indiana 46711   Clotilde.com

Backstitch to secure stitching, and press tuck toward center back. Pin or baste in place at waistline (Figure 2).

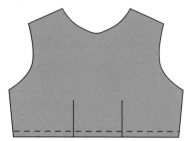

Figure 2

2. Stitch bodice fronts (T) to bodice back (U) at shoulder seams. Press toward back.

3. Bind neckline edge and sleeve hems with ½-inch contrasting double-fold bias tape. Using contrasting thread, topstitch three times around neckline edge and sleeve hems (Figure 3).

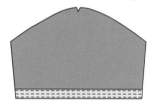

Figure 3

4. Stitch sleeves (L) to dress bodice.

5. Stitch skirt backs (W) together at center back (Figure 4). Press seam to one side.

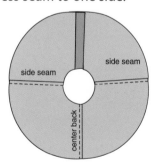

Figure 4

6. Stitch skirt fronts (V) to skirt back (W) at side seams. Press seams toward skirt front (Figure 4).

7. With right sides together, pin the skirt to the bodice, matching front edges and side seams (Figure 5). Sew and press seam toward skirt.

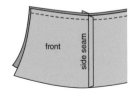

Figure 5

8. Stitch a ¼-inch double-turned hem down both front edges of dress.

9. Apply ½-inch single-fold bias tape to hem the Wrap Dress skirt.

10. Fold 2 x 22-inch strip for belt in half, right sides together, and stitch lengthwise edge. Turn right side out. Center seam on one side and press. Tuck ¼ inch to inside on short ends; press and pin to hold. Topstitch belt around all edges.

11. Place pin 6" from end of belt. Attach belt to right center front at pin and secure by stitching button at that point (Figure 6). Remove pins.

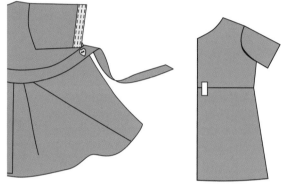

Figure 6   **Figure 7**

12. Apply hook side of one fusible hook-and-loop tape fastener to right side of left front bodice, centered over waistline (Figure 7). Apply loop side of tape to wrong side of right front bodice, also centered over waistline. Overlap dress front and fasten hook-and-loop tape. Position and apply three more fusible hook-and-loop tape fasteners evenly spaced to hold overlap in place.

13. To complete Wrap Dress, sew one button at center front of each sleeve (Figure 8a), two buttons above belt and three buttons below belt, evenly spaced (Figure 8b). ❖

Figure 8a

Figure 8b

Floral Drop-Waist Dress

Materials
- 2 coordinating fat quarters (A, B)
- 2 inches ¾-inch-wide heat-activated fusible hook-and-loop tape
- 3 (½-inch) buttons
- Contrasting color general-purpose thread
- Basic sewing supplies and equipment

Cutting
Use pattern templates X, Y, Z, AA and BB (pages 50-51). Transfer all pattern markings to fabric.

From Fat Quarter A:
- Cut one front bodice (X) on fold.
- Cut two back bodice (Y), reverse one.
- Cut two sleeve (Z), reverse one.
- Cut two 3½ x 15-inch strips for skirt.

From Fat Quarter B:
- Cut one bodice placket (AA).
- Cut four sleeve cuffs (BB), reverse 2.
- Cut two 3 x 15-inch strips for skirt hemline accent.
- Cut three 1 x 9½-inch strips for bias tape (see page 38, Making Bias Tape).
- Cut two 1½ x 15-inch strips for waistband.

From ¾-inch-wide heat-activated fusible hook-and-loop tape:
- Cut four ½ x ¾-inch hook-and-loop fasteners.

Assembly
Stitch right sides together using a ¼-inch seam unless otherwise specified. Refer to General Instructions (page 4) for finishing all seams, and for the following construction techniques: Topstitching, Bias-Tape Bound Edges, Sleeves, Basting, Fastener Application.

1. Stitch bodice front (X) to bodice backs (Y) at shoulder seams. Press seams to back.

2. Fold bodice placket (AA) in half, right sides together, and stitch lengthwise edge. Turn right side out. Center seam on one side and press. Position and pin bodice placket (AA) over center front of bodice. Topstitch down either side (Figure 1).

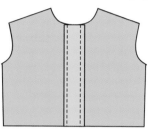

Figure 1

3. Use one 9½-inch bias strip to bind neckline edge.

4. Stitch sleeves to bodice.

5. Stitch two sleeve cuff (BB) pieces together on both short ends and one long end. Trim seams and corners. Turn right side out and press.

6. Pin cuff to sleeve bottom, matching large and small dots. There will be approximately ¼ inch between ends of cuff. Baste in place (Figure 2).

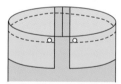

Figure 2

7. Press a second 9½-inch bias strip flat. Fold strip in half, right sides together, to make a ½-inch-wide bias strip; press. Fold one short end ¼ inch to wrong side and press (Figure 3). Beginning with folded short end and matching raw edges, position and pin bias tape around bottom of cuff/sleeve. Stitch in place (Figure 4). Trim seam allowance only. Press bias and seam toward sleeve. Hand-stitch in place. Repeat for second sleeve.

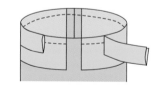

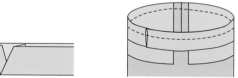

¼"

Figure 3   **Figure 4**

8. Stitch hemline accent strips together along short ends. Press seam open. Fold strip in half lengthwise, wrong sides together, and press. Stitch skirt strips together along short ends. Press seam open.

9. Stitch accent strip to skirt bottom edge using a ½-inch seam. Press seam toward skirt. On right side, topstitch through all layers ⅜ inch from the seam line (Figure 5).

Figure 5

10. Mark and fold 1-inch pleats in skirt referring to Folding Pleats on page 19.

11. Sandwich bodice between waistband strips with waistbands right sides together (Figure 6). Stitch. Press waistband strips away from bodice. Topstitch ⅛ inch from seam on waistband (Figure 7). Trim waistband strips to bodice width.

Figure 6

Figure 7

12. Pin bodice/waistband to skirt, adjusting pleats in skirt to match bodice/waistband if necessary. Stitch. Press seam toward waistband. Topstitch ⅛ inch from seam on waistband (Figure 8).

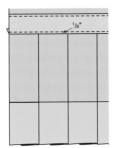

Figure 8

13. Bind back edges of dress with bias tape.

14. Apply four fusible hook-and-loop tape fasteners to back of dress.

15. To complete Floral Drop-Waist Dress, sew three buttons centered on front waistband (Figure 9). ❖

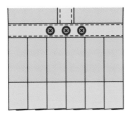

Figure 9

Folding Pleats

1. Mark pleats on wrong side of fabric (Figure 1).

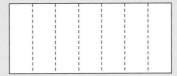

Figure 1

2. With top edge facing you, fold pleats by bringing marked pleat lines together. Pin pleat with fold to the right (Figure 2). Press.

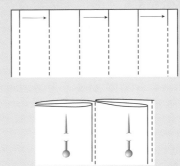

Figure 2

3. Baste across pleats at seam line to secure (Figure 3). Remove basting after stitching.

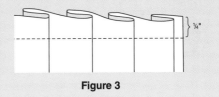

Figure 3

Suit Jacket & Skirt

Materials
- 2 coordinating fat quarters (A, B)
- 2 inches ¼-inch-wide elastic
- ½ inch ¾-inch-wide heat-activated fusible hook-and-loop tape
- 6 (½-inch) buttons
- Contrasting general-purpose thread
- Basic sewing supplies and equipment

Cutting
Use pattern templates L, FF, GG, HH and II (pages 41, 51-53), following cutting lines for Suit Jacket & Skirt on multiple-garment patterns. Transfer all pattern markings to fabric.

From fat quarter A:
- Cut two suit jacket fronts (FF), reverse one.
- Cut one suit jacket back (GG) on fold.
- Cut two sleeves (L), reverse one.
- Cut 1-inch-wide bias strips to total 25 inches in length (see page 38, Making Bias Strips).
- Cut two 2 x 18-inch strips for pleated skirt hemline accent.

From fat quarter B:
- Cut 1 skirt back (II) on fold.
- Cut 2 skirt fronts (HH), reverse one.
- Cut one 1¼ x 11½-inch strip for waistband.
- Cut two 1½ x 6-inch strips for sleeve accent.

Assembly
Stitch right sides together using a ¼-inch seam unless otherwise specified. Refer to General Instructions (page 4) for finishing all seams, and for the following construction techniques: Topstitching, Basting, Backstitching.

Suit Jacket
1. Stitch jacket fronts (FF) to jacket back (GG) at shoulder seams. Press seams toward back. Stitch 1-inch-wide bias tape to neckline front edges of jacket. Turn to inside edge and hand-stitch in place.

2. Press ¼ inch to wrong side of one lengthwise edge of one sleeve accent strip. Stitch unpressed edge of strip to bottom of sleeve (Figure 1). Press accent strip away from sleeve. Turn to wrong side of sleeve and align pressed edge to seam. Hand-stitch in place (Figure 2).

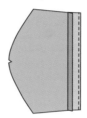 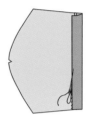

Figure 1   **Figure 2**

3. Stitch sleeves to jacket referring to General Instructions.

4. Cut a 3½-inch length of 1-inch-wide bias tape. Press ¼ inch of each end to wrong side. Pin to jacket back at marked casing position. Topstitch close to both lengthwise edges (Figure 3).

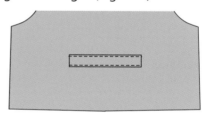

Figure 3

5. Thread 2-inch piece of ¼-inch-wide elastic through casing. Pin both ends securely just inside casing. Topstitch across ends catching elastic to secure (Figure 4).

Figure 4

6. Press ¼ inch of jacket hem accent strip to wrong side along both ends and one lengthwise edge.

House of White Birches, Berne, Indiana 46711   Clotilde.com

Stitch unpressed raw edge to jacket hem, matching ends to jacket front edges (Figure 5). Adjust, if necessary, by refolding ends.

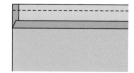

Figure 5

7. Fold and pin accent strip to wrong side of jacket, matching fold to seam. Hand-stitch in place and press (Figure 6).

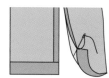

Figure 6

8. Stitch three coordinating ½-inch buttons to both sides of jacket, beginning at neckline curve and spacing approximately ½ inch apart (Figure 7).

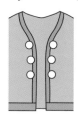

Figure 7

Suit Skirt

1. With wrong sides together, stitch ¼ inch from center front fold of skirt front (HH) along tuck-stitching line. Press tuck to left. Baste at waist and hemline to hold.

2. Stitch darts into front of skirt (Figure 8). Stitch the center back seam of skirt to X. Backstitch to secure. Press seam open, pressing back unstitched sides also (Figure 9).

Figure 8

Figure 9

3. Stitch skirt front (HH) and skirt backs (II) along side seams. Press toward back.

4. Press ¼ inch to wrong side on one lengthwise edge and both ends of waistband. Pin and stitch unpressed edge to skirt, matching end to right side of skirt back opening (Figure 10). Left side should extend approximately ½ inch beyond skirt back seam.

Figure 10

5. Fold and pin pressed edge to wrong side of skirt, matching pressed edge to seam. Hand-stitch in place as in Step 7 of Jacket, stitching ends closed also.

6. Apply one heat-activated fusible hook-and-loop tape fastener to the waistband, following manufacturer's instructions (Figure 11).

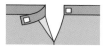

Figure 11

7. Stitch two hemline accent strips together at both ends, forming a circle, press seams open. Fold the strip in half lengthwise and press. Pleat in 1-inch pleats (see page 19, Folding Pleats).

8. Pin strip to bottom edge of skirt, adjusting pleats to match hemline width. Stitch and press seam toward skirt. Topstitch ¼ inch from seam line. ❖

Cropped Jacket & Gathered Pants

Materials
- 2 coordinating fat quarters (A, B)
- 1 package coordinating ¼-inch-wide single-fold bias tape
- 11 inches ¼-inch-wide elastic
- 1 inch ¾-inch-wide heat-activated fusible hook-and-loop tape
- 2 (½-inch) buttons
- Basic sewing supplies and equipment

Cutting
Use pattern templates L, I, JJ, KK, LL, MM and NN (pages 41, 46, 53-55), following cutting lines for Cropped Jacket and Gathered Pants on multiple-garment patterns. Transfer all pattern markings to fabric.

From fat quarter A:
- Cut two cropped jacket fronts (JJ), reverse one.
- Cut one cropped jacket back (KK) on fold.
- Cut two sleeves (L), reverse one.
- Cut one 2 x 22-inch strip for jacket hemline accent.

From fat quarter B:
- Cut two cropped jacket fronts (JJ), reverse one.
- Cut one cropped jacket back facing (LL) on fold.
- Cut two gathered pants upper fronts (MM), reverse one.
- Cut two gathered pants lower fronts (NN), reverse one.
- Cut two pants backs (I), reverse one.
- Cut one 1 x 22-inch strip for pants hem binding.

From ¾-inch-wide heat-activated fusible hook-and-loop tape:
- Cut two ½ x ¾-inch fasteners.

Assembly
Stitch right sides together using a ¼-inch seam unless otherwise specified. Refer to General Instructions (page 4) for finishing all seams, and for the following construction techniques: Basting, Bias-Tape Bound Edges, Bias-Tape Hems & Casings, Sleeves, Gathering, Topstitching, Fastener Application.

Cropped Jacket

1. With jacket back (KK) folded right sides together, stitch along tuck-stitching line, leaving seam open between Xs (Figure 1).

Figure 1

2. Press seam flat creating tuck at center back. Baste tuck at neck and hem to hold (Figure 2).

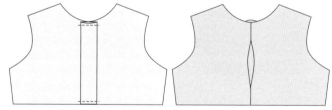

Figure 2

3. Stitch fat-quarter A jacket fronts (JJ) to jacket back (KK) at shoulder seams. Press seams toward back.

4. Bind jacket back facing (LL) with bias tape along outer edge.

5. Stitch jacket back facing (LL) to fat-quarter B jacket fronts (JJ) at shoulder seams to create lining. Press seams toward front.

6. Stitch lining to jacket around neckline and along front opening. Trim corners, turn right side out and press.

7. Stitch bias tape hem to sleeves. Stitch sleeves to jacket.

8. Turn short ends of hemline accent strip ¼ inch to wrong side and press. Press strip in half lengthwise, wrong sides together. Gather and stitch to jacket hem.

9. Press seam toward jacket. Sew two rows topstitching around jacket hem, neck and front edges (Figure 3).

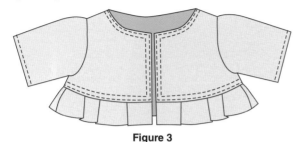

Figure 3

10. Apply two fusible hook-and-loop fasteners to the jacket front.

11. Sew two ½-inch buttons to the right side of jacket front centered between neckline and jacket hemline (Figure 4).

Figure 4

Gathered Pants

1. Gather (see page 4, Gathering) lower front pants (NN). Stitch to upper front pants (MM). Press seam toward upper front pants.

2. Stitch completed pants fronts to pants backs (I) along side seams. Press seams toward back (Figure 5).

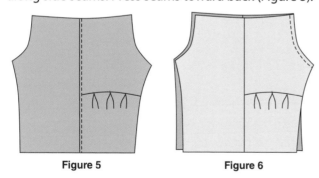

Figure 5   **Figure 6**

3. Stitch pants center front seam. Press to one side (Figure 6).

4. Create an elastic casing by turning ⅛ inch to wrong side along waistline. Press. Turn to wrong side again along casing line. Press and pin along first fold to hold. Stitch close to first fold line (Figure 7).

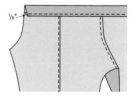

Figure 7

5. Thread elastic through casing. Pin ends of elastic even with back seam of pants and stitch to secure (Figure 8).

Figure 8

6. Press 1 x 22-inch strip for pants hem binding ¼ inch to wrong side along both lengthwise edges. With right side of binding to wrong side of pants legs hem, pin binding to pants legs hem, trimming to fit. Stitch along fold (Figure 9).

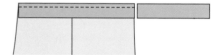

Figure 9

7. Press binding to pants right side, folding over hem edges. Topstitch on right side along folded edge to bind hem (Figure 10).

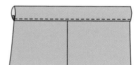

Figure 10

8. Stitch pants center back seam. Press to one side. Sew inner leg seams, matching center front and back seams, to complete pants. ❖

Shirtdress

Materials

- 1 fat quarter
- 1 package coordinating ½-inch-wide single fold bias tape
- 1½ inches ¾-inch-wide heat-activated fusible hook-and-loop tape
- 4 (½-inch) buttons
- Contrasting general purpose thread
- Basic sewing supplies and equipment

Cutting

Use pattern templates J, K, L, M and N (pages 41, 43–44), following cutting lines for Shirtdress on multiple-garment patterns. Transfer all pattern markings to fabric.

From fat quarter:
- Cut two shirtdress fronts (J), reverse one.
- Cut one shirtdress back (K) on fold.
- Cut two sleeves (L), reverse one.
- Cut two shirtdress facings (N), reverse one.
- Cut two shirtdress collars (M) on fold.
- Cut two 2¾ x 2¾-inch squares for pocket.

From ¾-inch-wide heat-activated fusible hook-and-loop tape:
- Cut three ½ x ¾-inch fasteners.

Assembly

Stitch right sides together using a ¼-inch seam unless otherwise specified. Refer to General Instructions (page 4) for finishing all seams, and for the following construction techniques: Collars, Facings, Bias-Tape Hems & Casings, Double-Turned ¼-Inch Hem, Sleeves, Fastener Application.

1. Folding right sides of shirtdress back (K) together, sew along tuck-stitching line at center back to X. Press tuck to one side. Using a contrasting thread, topstitch from neckline down stitching line, across the tuck at X to the fold, and then up to the neckline (Figure 1).

Figure 1

2. Stitch Shirtdress fronts (J) and back (K) together at shoulder seams. Press seams open.

3. Construct and stitch collar (M) to neckline.

4. Construct and stitch facings (N) to Shirtdress.

5. Stitch a bias-tape hem into Shirtdress hemline, trimming bias approximately ½ inch longer than needed and folding ends to wrong side before applying to Shirtdress.

6. Sew pocket squares right sides together along one side. Turn so wrong sides are together, press. Topstitch ⅛ inch from seam line and again ¼ inch from first stitching.

7. Turn remaining raw edges under ¼ inch. Position pocket on left front, approximately 1¼ inches from bottom. Sew in place ⅛ inch from edge on sides and bottom, leaving top open.

8. Stitch double-turned hem in each sleeve, turning under ⅛ inch. Stitch sleeves to shirtdress.

9. Fold 2 x 22-inch strip for belt in half, right sides together, and stitch lengthwise edge. Turn right side out. Center seam on one side and press. Tuck ¼ inch to inside on short ends; press, and pin to hold. Topstitch belt around all edges.

10. Mark center of belt length. Position belt center approximately 3½ inches from neckline on center back seam and topstitch to shirtdress (Figure 2).

Figure 2

11. Apply three fusible hook-and-loop tape fasteners to the Shirtdress front.

12. Stitch one ½-inch button to center top of pocket. Stitch three ½-inch buttons to right side of Shirtdress front opening, spacing evenly. ❖

House of White Birches, Berne, Indiana 46711   Clotilde.com

Color Blocked A-Line Dress

Materials
- 2 contrasting fat quarters (A, B)
- 11 (¼-inch) buttons
- 1½ inches ¾-inch-wide heat-activated fusible hook-and-loop tape
- Basic sewing supplies and equipment

Cutting
Use pattern templates L, QQ, RR, SS, TT and UU (pages 41, 56-57), following cutting lines for A-Line Dress on multiple-garment patterns. Transfer all pattern markings to fabric.

From fat quarter A:
- Cut two dress fronts (QQ), reverse one.
- Cut two dress backs (RR), reverse one.
- Cut two sleeves (L), reverse one.
- Cut two dress pockets (SS).

From fat quarter B:
- Cut two dress front facings (TT) on fold.
- Cut four dress back facings (UU), reverse two.
- Cut four 1½ x 22-inch strips. Subcut into two 6-inch lengths for sleeve hems, two 8½-inch lengths for center front edging, two 4¼-inch lengths for pocket accents and one 12-inch length for belt. Remaining strip length will be used for dress hemline.

From ¾-inch-wide heat-activated fusible hook-and-loop tape:
- Cut three ½ x ¾-inch fasteners.

Assembly
Stitch right sides together using a ¼-inch seam unless otherwise specified. Refer to General Instructions (page 4) for finishing all seams and for the following specific construction techniques: Basting, Topstitching, Sleeves, Fastener Application.

1. Press ¼ inch to wrong side of the lengthwise edge of each of the center front edging strips. Stitch unpressed edges of edging strips to center front edges of both dress fronts (QQ as shown in Figure 1. Press seams toward edging strips.

Figure 1

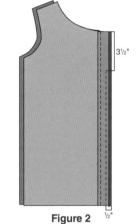

Figure 2

2. Using a ½-inch seam, stitch dress front/edging strip pieces together leaving seam open from neckline to 3½ inches from neckline (Figure 2). Press seam open. Hand stitch the pressed edge of edging strip on both sides along seam line (Figure 3). Press.

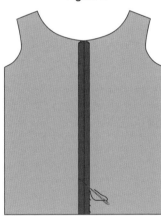

Figure 3

3. Stitch dress front (QQ) and backs (RR) together at shoulder seams. Press seams open.

4. Stitch facings (TT) and (UU) together at shoulder seams. Press seams open. Finish edges.

5. Pin facings right sides together and stitch along center backs and neckline, matching shoulder seams (Figure 4). Trim corners and turn right sides out. Press.

Figure 4

6. Baste facings together ¼ inch from open edges. Sandwich and pin dress between facings at neckline and center back making dress edges touch basting (Figure 5). Baste facings in place. Stitch over facing raw edge with a satin stitch. Adjust stitch width to catch and cover both garment outside and inside edges of facings, while still remaining narrow (Figure 6). Remove all basting.

Figure 5   **Figure 6**

7. Sew accent strips to top edge of each pocket, trimming to fit. Turn to wrong side. Press ¼ inch of strip to wrong side. Position pressed edge on seam and hand-stitch in place (Figure 7). Press.

Figure 7

8. Press ¼ inch to wrong side on sides and bottom of pocket.

9. Pin pockets to dress front where indicated on pattern template. Topstitch along sides and bottom edges of pockets.

10. Sew accent strips to bottom of each sleeve, referring to Step 9 and Figure 7. Stitch sleeves to dress.

11. Measure hemline length and cut remaining accent strip that length plus ½ inch.

12. Press ¼ inch to wrong side of hemline accent strip on one lengthwise edge and both short ends. Matching strip end to dress center back, stitch unpressed lengthwise edge of strip, right side to wrong side of dress, at hemline.

13. Press strip to dress right side and topstitch along pressed lengthwise edge and ends.

14. Fold 1½ x 12-inch strip for belt in half right sides together and stitch lengthwise edge. Turn right side out. Center seam on one side and press. Cut two 6-inch pieces. Topstitch sections around all edges.

15. Turn under each of the ends and stitch each belt section to dress where indicated on pattern template. Stitch a button at each end (Figure 8).

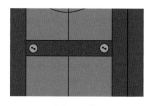

Figure 8   **Figure 9**

16. Apply three fusible hook-and-loop tape fasteners to the A-line dress back.

17. Stitch five ¼-inch buttons evenly space between the shoulder seams along front neckline accent, referring to Figure 9. Sew one button to each pocket as shown. ❖

Wool Dress Coat

Materials
- 2 (12 x 18-inch) rectangles wool blend felt
- 1 coordinating fat quarter
- 4 (9 x 12-inch) sheets fusible web
- 2 (½-inch) buttons
- 1 package coordinating ¼-inch-wide single-fold bias tape
- 1 inch ¾-inch-wide heat-activated fusible hook-and-loop tape
- Contrasting color general-purpose thread
- Basic sewing supplies and equipment

Fabric Preparation
Cut a 4 x 8-inch piece from one wool felt rectangle.

Apply fusible web to the remainder of the wool felt rectangle, and to the second whole wool felt rectangle. Position the fused felt pieces web-side down onto the wrong side of the coordinating fat quarter and fuse in place. Trim the fat quarter even with the felt pieces.

Cutting
Use pattern templates A, B, C, D, E, F and G (pages 58-60). Transfer all pattern markings to fabric.

From 4 x 8-inch wool felt rectangle:
- Cut two coat pockets (G).

From the partial fused felt piece:
- Cut one coat back (B) on the fold.
- Cut one back collar (D) on the fold.
- Cut one left collar (E).
- Cut one right collar (F).

From whole fused felt piece:
- Cut two coat fronts (A), reversing one.
- Cut two coat sleeves (C), reversing one.

From ¾-inch-wide heat-activated fusible hook-and-loop tape:
- Cut two ½ x ¾-inch fasteners.

House of White Birches, Berne, Indiana 46711   Clotilde.com

Assembly

Stitch right sides together using a ¼-inch seam unless otherwise specified. Refer to General Instructions (page 4) for finishing all seams, and for the following construction techniques: Topstitching, Fastener Application.

1. Folding right sides of coat back (B) together, sew along tuck-stitching line at center back from neckline to X. Press tuck to one side. Using a contrasting thread, topstitch from neckline down stitching line, across the tuck at X to the fold , and then up to neckline (Figure 1).

Figure 1

2. Sew coat fronts (A) and coat back (B) together at shoulder seams. Press seams toward front and topstitch through all thicknesses close to seam allowance edge.

3. Topstitch along outside edges of coat front and coat back hemlines using a contrasting color thread. Trim close to the stitching line using pinking shears or scalloped-edge scissors (Figure 2).

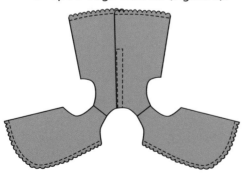

Figure 2

4. Pin collar sections (D, E, F) together and stitch. Press seams toward back collar and sew through all thicknesses. Topstitch along outside edges of collar using a contrasting color thread, and trimming as in Step 3. Stitch collar to coat neckline with collar fat-quarter side to coat felt side, matching shoulder seams.

5. Pin unfolded bias tape edge right sides together with collar along neck edge and sew. Fold bias tape to the inside and hand-stitch to secure (Figure 3).

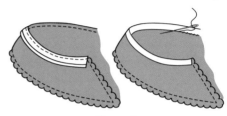

Figure 3

6. Pin pockets (G) next to the side seams at the position marked on coat front (A) pattern. Topstitch, referring to Figure 4.

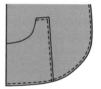

Figure 4

7. Topstitch sleeve hemline, and trim as in Step 3 (Figure 5). Sew sleeves to coat.

Figure 5

8. Apply fusible hook-and-loop tape fasteners to front opening, approximately 1½ and 4 inches from neckline.

9. Sew ½-inch decorative buttons to the right side of the coat front over the hook-and-loop tape positions. ❖

Asian-Inspired Pajamas

Materials
- 3 coordinating Asian-print fat quarters (A, B, C)
- 1 package coordinating ¼-inch-wide bias tape
- 11 inches ¼-inch-wide elastic
- 1 x ¾-inch-wide heat-activated fusible hook-and-loop tape
- 3 (¾-inch) bar buttons
- Basic sewing supplies and equipment

Cutting
Use pattern templates O, P, Q, R and S (pages 60-63). Transfer all pattern markings to fabric.

From Fat Quarter A:
- Cut two pajama top fronts (O), reverse one.
- Cut one pajama top back (P) on fold.

From Fat Quarter B:
- Cut two pajama top front facings (Q), reverse one.
- Cut one pajama top back facing (R) on fold.
- Cut a total of 70 inches of 1-inch-wide bias strips (see page 38, Making Bias Tape)

From Fat Quarter C:
- Cut four pajama pants (S), reversing two.

From ¾-inch-wide heat-activated fusible hook-and-loop tape:
- Cut two ½ x ¾-inch fasteners.

Assembly
Stitch right sides together using a ¼-inch seam unless otherwise specified. Refer to General Instructions (page 4) for finishing all seams and for the following construction techniques: Facings, Double-Turned ¼-Inch Hem, Fastener Application.

Pajama Top
1. Stitch pajama top fronts (O) and back (P) together at shoulder seams. Press seam to back.

2. Construct and stitch facings to pajama top.

3. Stitch a double-turned ¼-inch hem onto the bottoms of the pajama top and the sleeves.

4. Stitch underarm seams. Press to back.

5. Apply two fusible hook-and-loop tape fasteners to front opening. Position fasteners approximately 2½ inches and 5½ inches from the shoulder seam.

6. Sew three ½-inch bar buttons evenly spaced along right side of the pajama front edge (Figure 1).

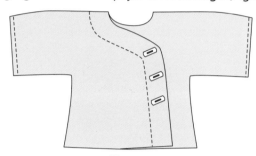

Figure 1

Pajama Pants
1. Use bias tape made from fat quarter B (see page 38) to bind pajama pants (S) hems and side seams to ½ inch above the X (Figure 2).

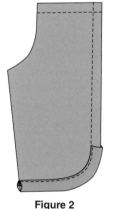

Figure 2   Figure 3

2. Stitch two pajama pants (S) pieces right sides together along side seams using a ½-inch seam, and stopping at X (Figure 3). Repeat for remaining two pajama pants (S) pieces.

House of White Birches, Berne, Indiana 46711 Clotilde.com

3. Stitch pants center front seam (Figure 4). Press to right.

Figure 4

4. Finish the top raw edge of pants. Press to wrong side along casing fold line. Stitch ⅜ inch from folded edge to create a casing for elastic (Figure 5).

Figure 5

5. Thread elastic through casing. Pin ends of elastic even with back seam of pants and stitch to secure (Figure 6).

Figure 6

6. Stitch pants center back seam. Press to left. Matching center front and back seams, stitch inner leg seam to complete pants. ❖

Making Bias Tape

Make your own bias tape to add a distinctive flair to any project. Instructions are for ¼-inch finished-size bias tape.

1. Fold fabric diagonally so crosswise grain straight edge is parallel to selvage or lengthwise grain. Cut fabric along this fold line to mark the true bias (Figure 1).

Figure 1

2. Using a clear ruler, mark successive bias lines 1 inch wide. Carefully cut along lines. Handle edges carefully to avoid stretching (Figure 2).

Figure 2

3. Sew short ends of strips together as shown in Figure 3.

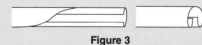

Figure 3

4. Fold strip in half lengthwise, wrong sides together. Press.

5. Open out with wrong side up. Fold each edge to center fold and press. Fold in half again and press.

Versatile Blouse

Materials
- 1 fat quarter
- 1 package matching ¼-inch-wide double-fold bias tape
- ⅜ yard lace trim, any width up to 2 inches
- 1½ inches ¾-inch-wide heat-activated fusible hook-and-loop tape
- Basic sewing supplies and equipment

Cutting
Use pattern templates L, OO and PP (page 41), following cutting lines for Versatile Blouse (either long or short sleeves) on multiple-garment patterns. Transfer all pattern markings to fabric.

From fat quarter:
- Cut one blouse front (OO) on fold.
- Cut two blouse backs (PP), reverse one.
- Cut two sleeves (L), reverse one (either long or short sleeve).

From ¾-inch-wide heat-activated fusible hook-and-loop tape:
- Cut three ½ x ¾-inch fasteners.

Assembly
Stitch right sides together using a ¼-inch seam unless otherwise specified. Refer to General Instructions (page 4) for finishing all seams, and for the following construction techniques: Bias-Tape Bound Edges, Sleeves, Topstitching, Double-Turned ¼-Inch Hem, Fastener Application.

1. Sew fitted bodice front (OO) and fitted bodice backs (PP) together at shoulder seams.

2. Bind neckline edge and sleeve hem edges with bias tape.

3. Stitch sleeves to bodice.

4. Pin lace to right side of bodice, matching lace to hemline (Figure 1).

Figure 1

House of White Birches, Berne, Indiana 46711   Clotilde.com

5. Topstitch top edge of lace to bodice, again referring to Figure 1.

6. On wrong side of bodice, closely trim bodice away from lace stitching (Figure 2).

Figure 2

7. Stitch a double-turned hem on center back edges, turning under ⅛ inch.

8. Apply three fusible hook-and-loop fasteners to bodice back. ❖

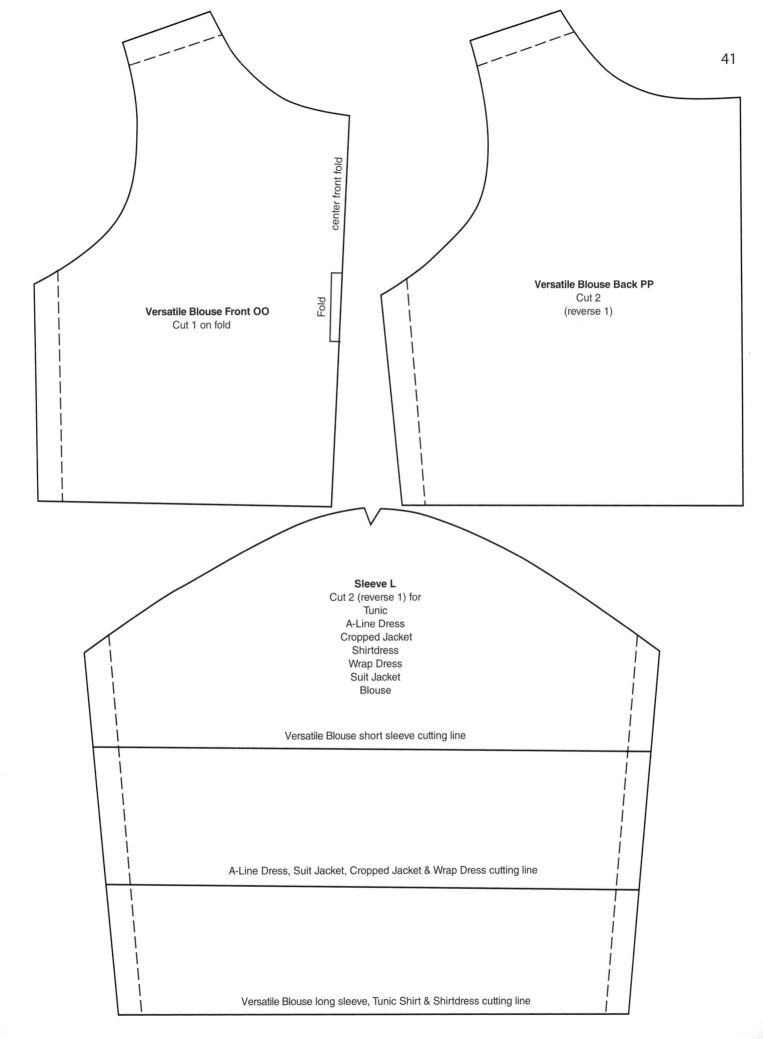

Versatile Blouse Front OO
Cut 1 on fold

center front fold

Fold

Versatile Blouse Back PP
Cut 2
(reverse 1)

Sleeve L
Cut 2 (reverse 1) for
Tunic
A-Line Dress
Cropped Jacket
Shirtdress
Wrap Dress
Suit Jacket
Blouse

Versatile Blouse short sleeve cutting line

A-Line Dress, Suit Jacket, Cropped Jacket & Wrap Dress cutting line

Versatile Blouse long sleeve, Tunic Shirt & Shirtdress cutting line

Glitzy Holiday Dress
Instructions on page 8

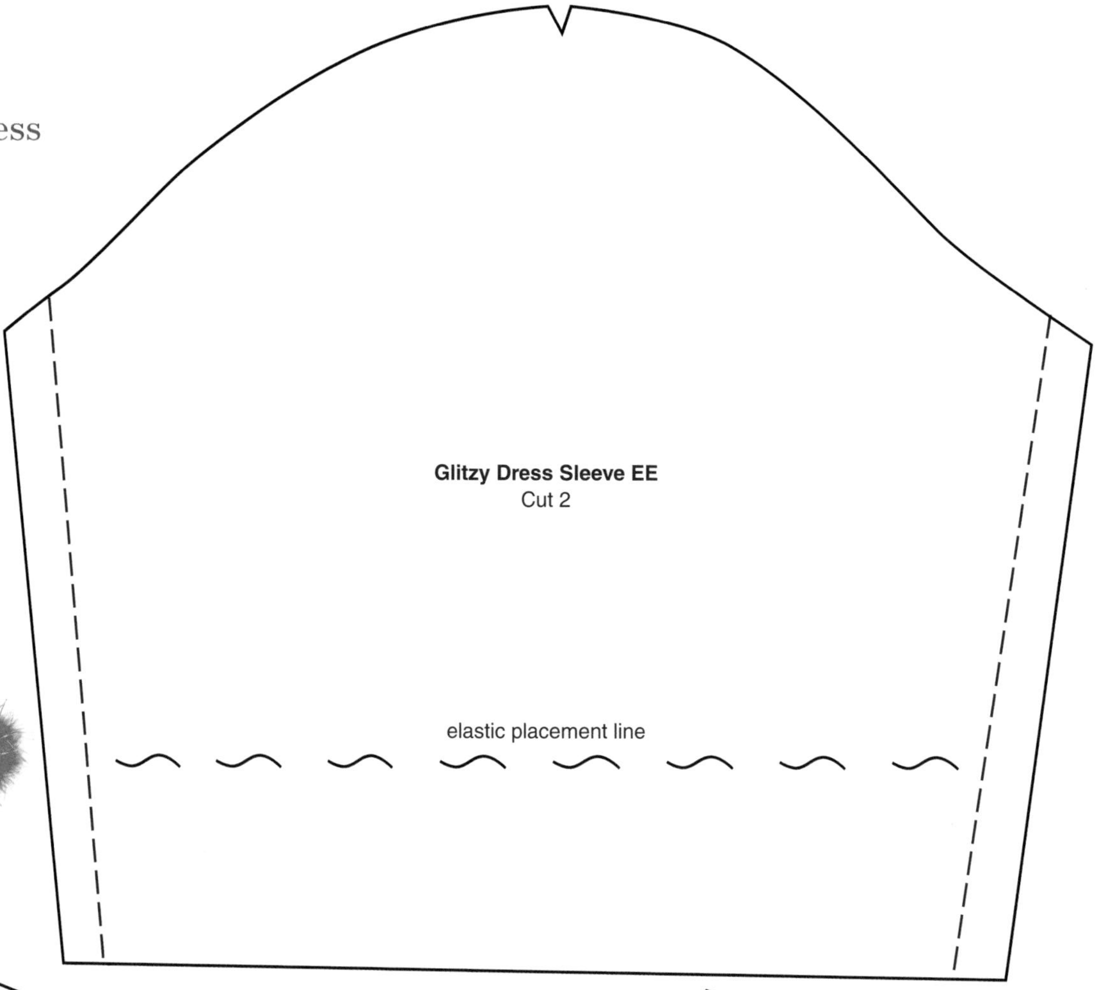

Glitzy Dress Sleeve EE
Cut 2

elastic placement line

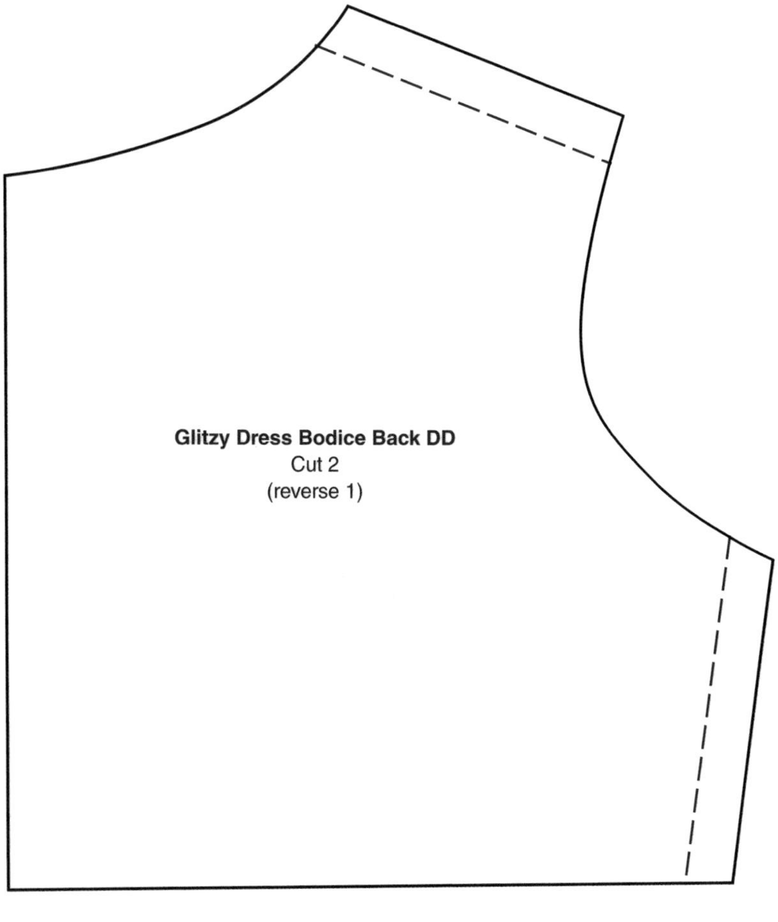

Glitzy Dress Bodice Back DD
Cut 2
(reverse 1)

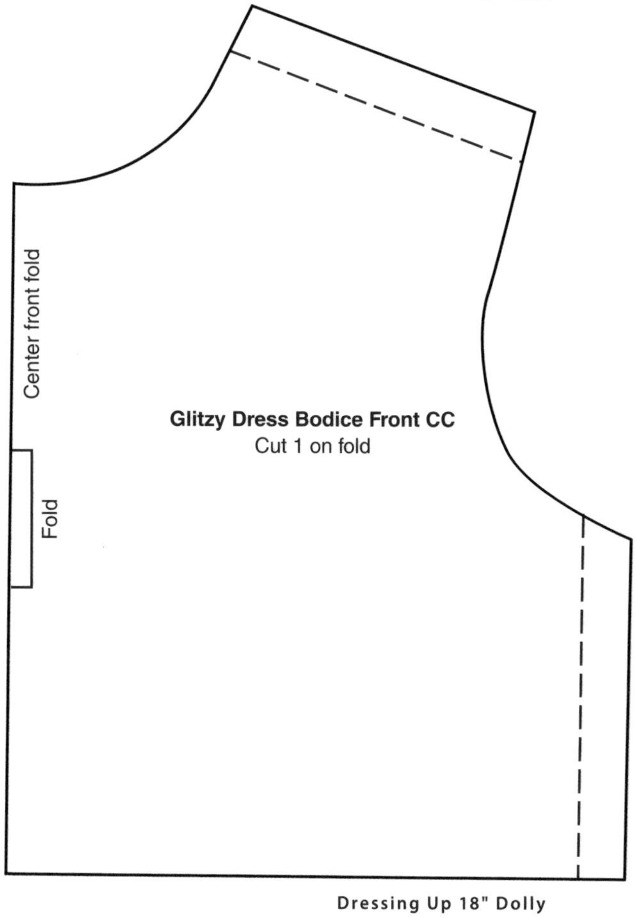

Center front fold

Fold

Glitzy Dress Bodice Front CC
Cut 1 on fold

Tunic & Pants

Instructions on page 10

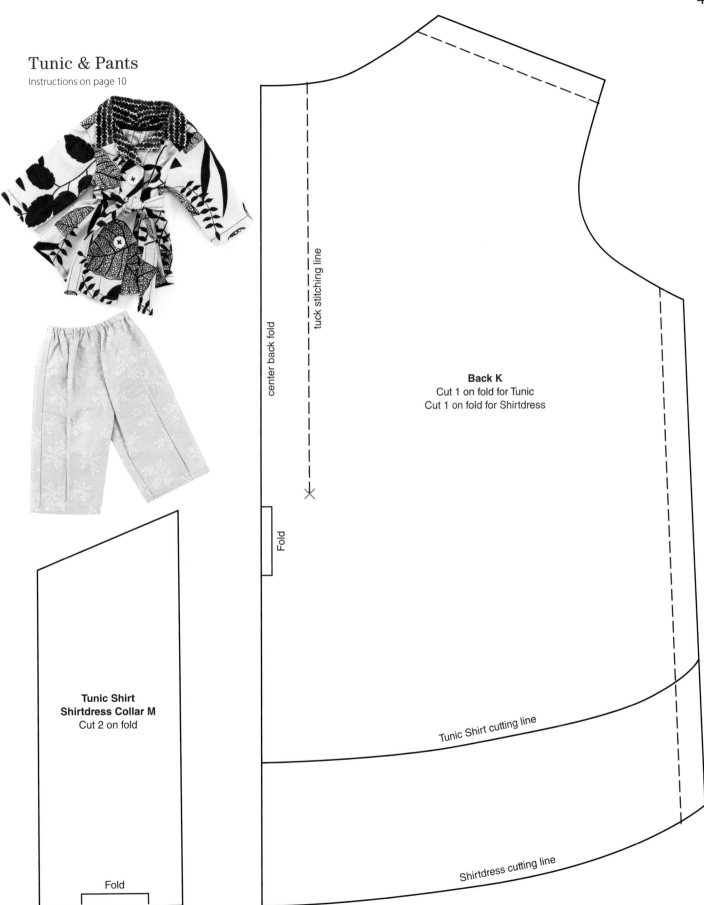

center back fold

tuck stitching line

Fold

Back K
Cut 1 on fold for Tunic
Cut 1 on fold for Shirtdress

Tunic Shirt cutting line

Shirtdress cutting line

Tunic Shirt
Shirtdress Collar M
Cut 2 on fold

Fold

House of White Birches, Berne, Indiana 46711   Clotilde.com

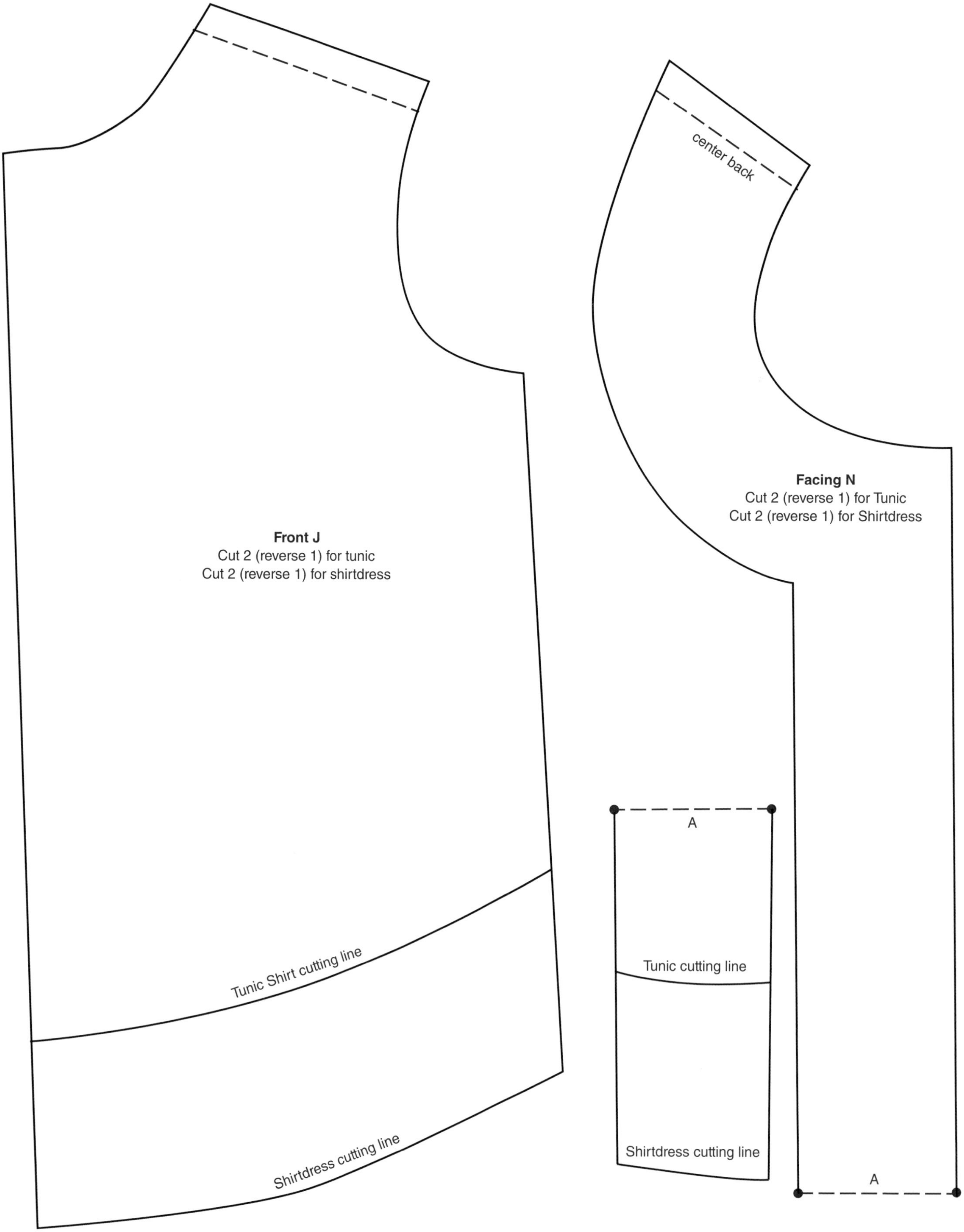

center back

Facing N
Cut 2 (reverse 1) for Tunic
Cut 2 (reverse 1) for Shirtdress

Front J
Cut 2 (reverse 1) for tunic
Cut 2 (reverse 1) for shirtdress

A

Tunic cutting line

Tunic Shirt cutting line

Shirtdress cutting line

A

Shirtdress cutting line

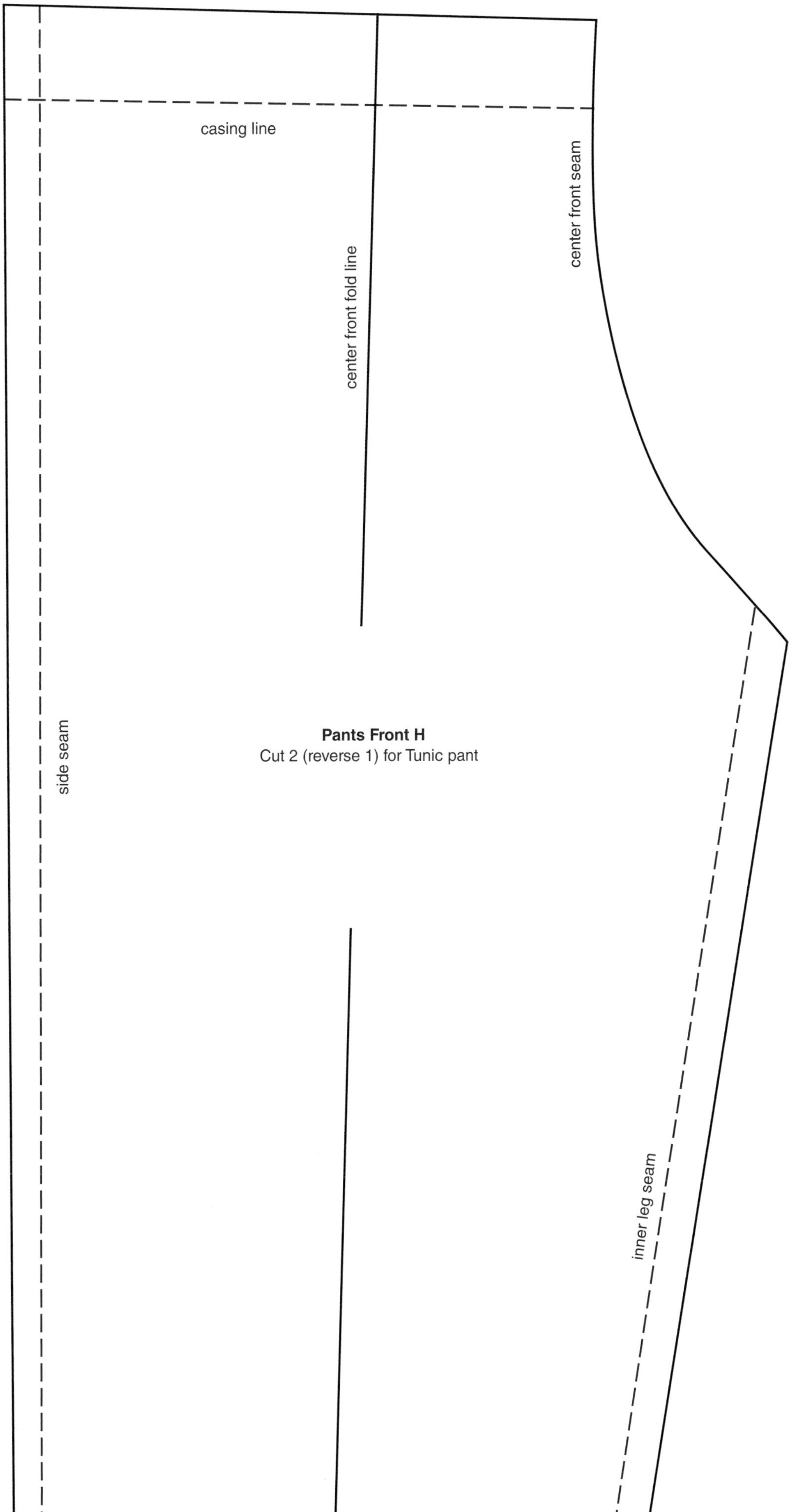

casing line

center front seam

center front fold line

side seam

Pants Front H
Cut 2 (reverse 1) for Tunic pant

inner leg seam

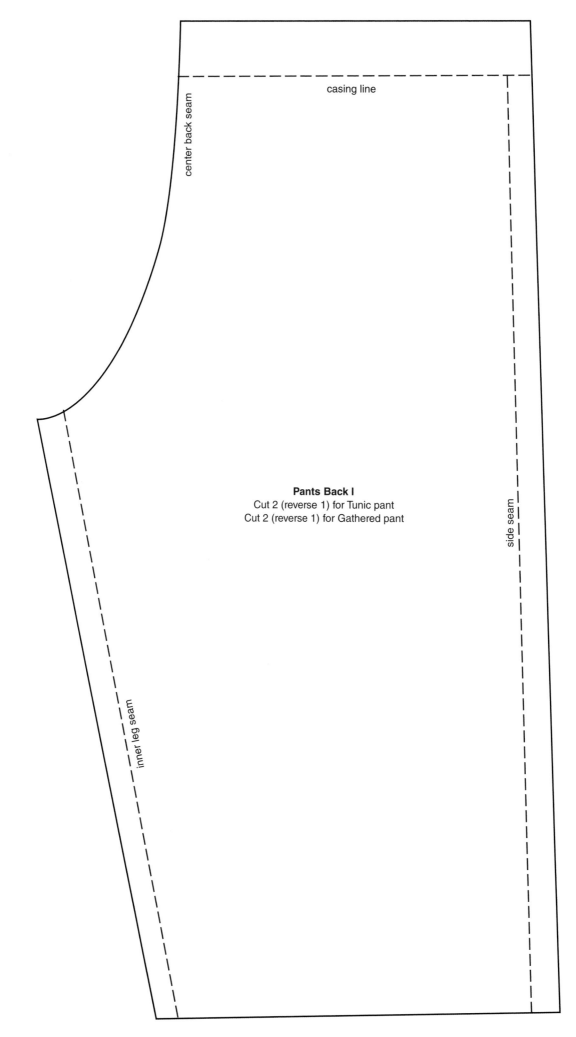

center back seam

casing line

side seam

Pants Back I
Cut 2 (reverse 1) for Tunic pant
Cut 2 (reverse 1) for Gathered pant

inner leg seam

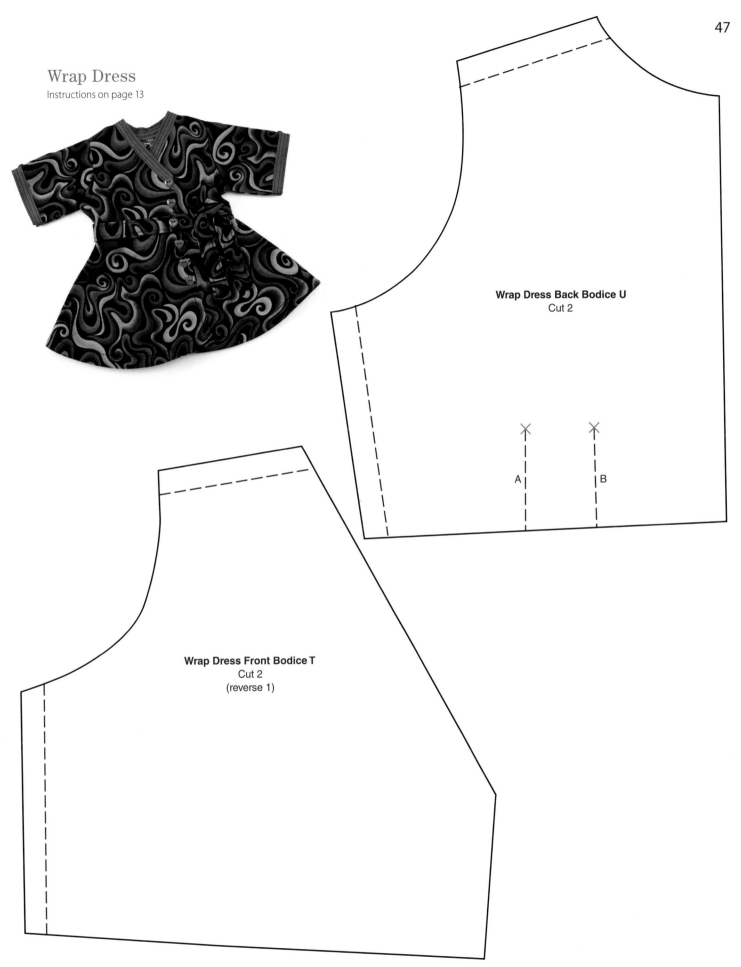

Wrap Dress
Instructions on page 13

Wrap Dress Back Bodice U
Cut 2

A   B

Wrap Dress Front Bodice T
Cut 2
(reverse 1)

House of White Birches, Berne, Indiana 46711   Clotilde.com

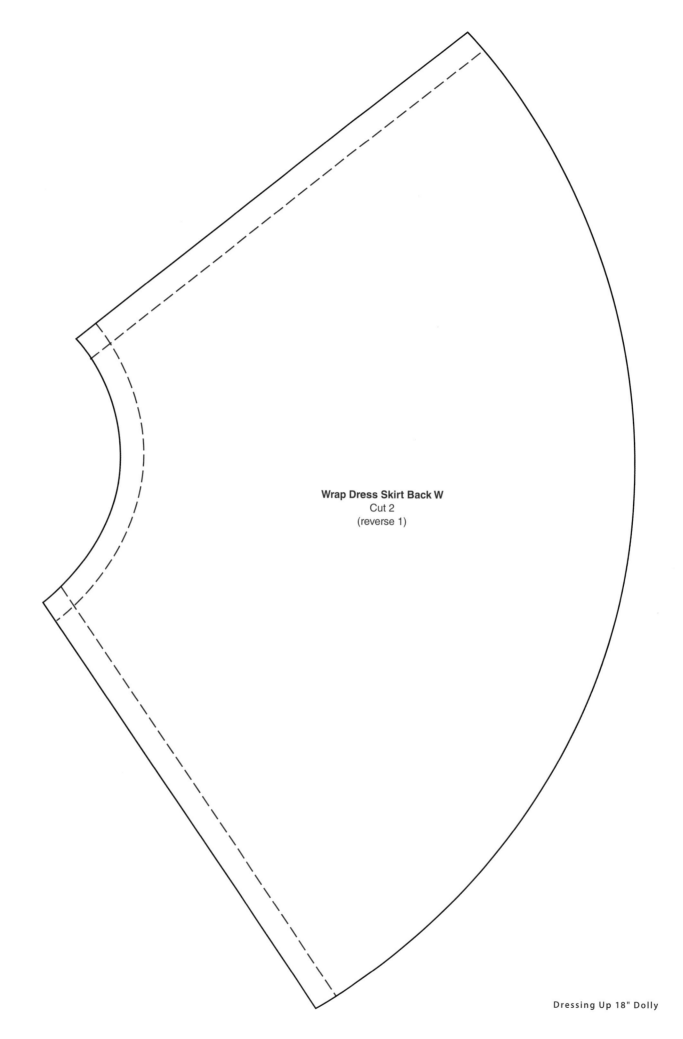

Wrap Dress Skirt Back W
Cut 2
(reverse 1)

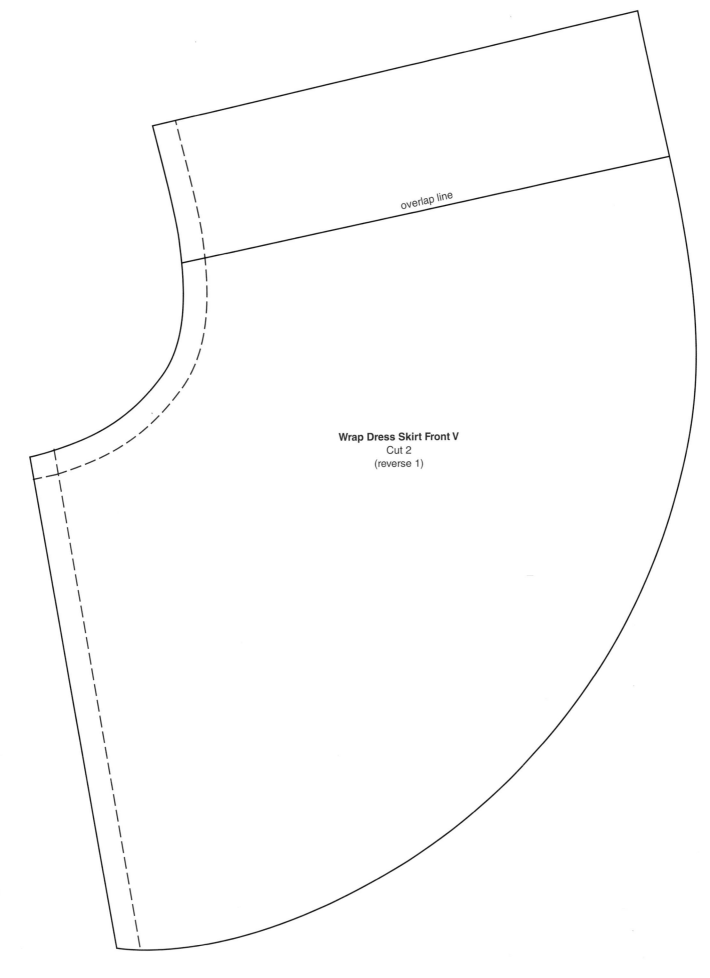

overlap line

Wrap Dress Skirt Front V
Cut 2
(reverse 1)

House of White Birches, Berne, Indiana 46711   Clotilde.com

Floral Drop-Waist Dress
Instructions on page 16

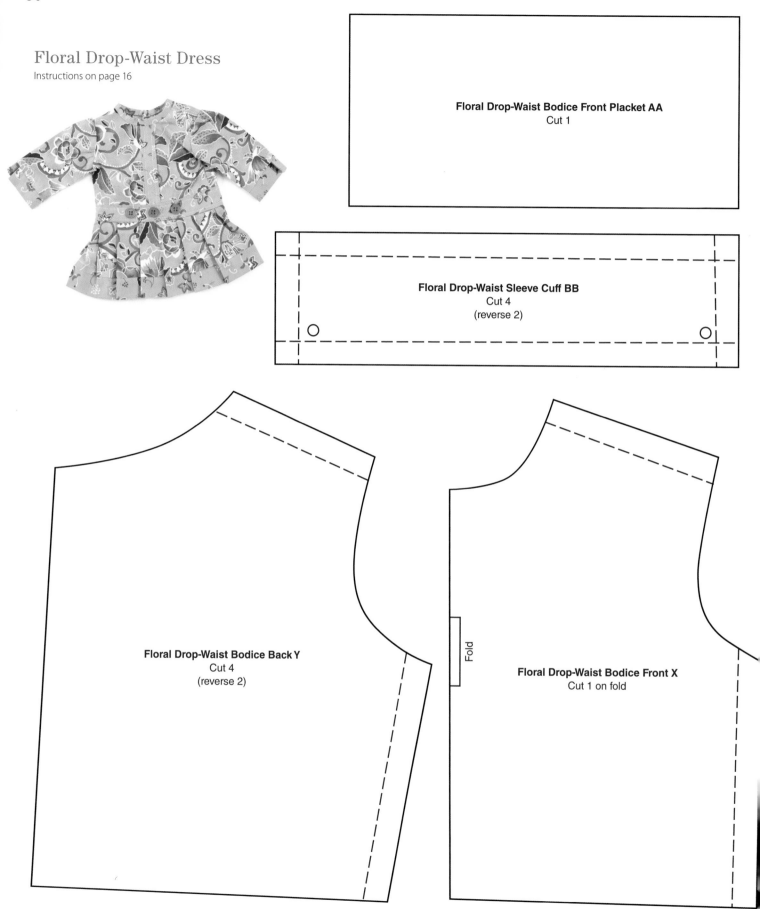

Floral Drop-Waist Bodice Front Placket AA
Cut 1

Floral Drop-Waist Sleeve Cuff BB
Cut 4
(reverse 2)

Floral Drop-Waist Bodice Back Y
Cut 4
(reverse 2)

Fold

Floral Drop-Waist Bodice Front X
Cut 1 on fold

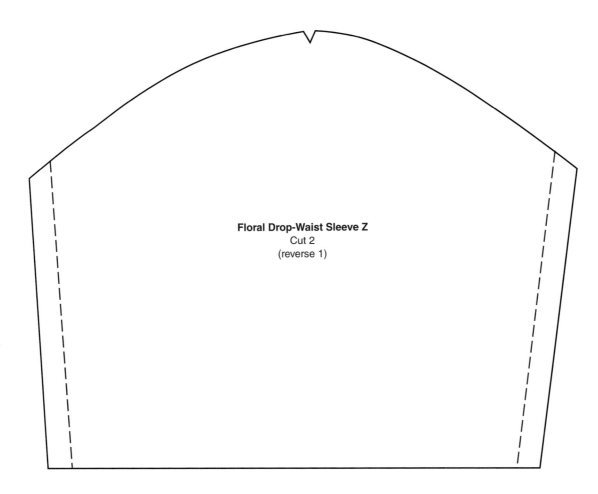

Floral Drop-Waist Sleeve Z
Cut 2
(reverse 1)

Suit Jacket & Skirt

Instructions on page 20

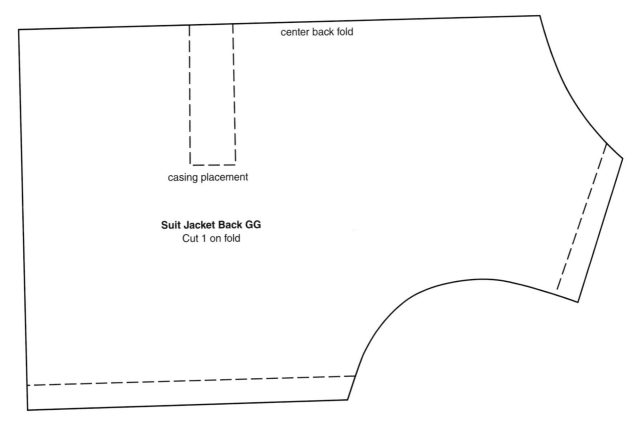

center back fold

casing placement

Suit Jacket Back GG
Cut 1 on fold

House of White Birches, Berne, Indiana 46711   Clotilde.com

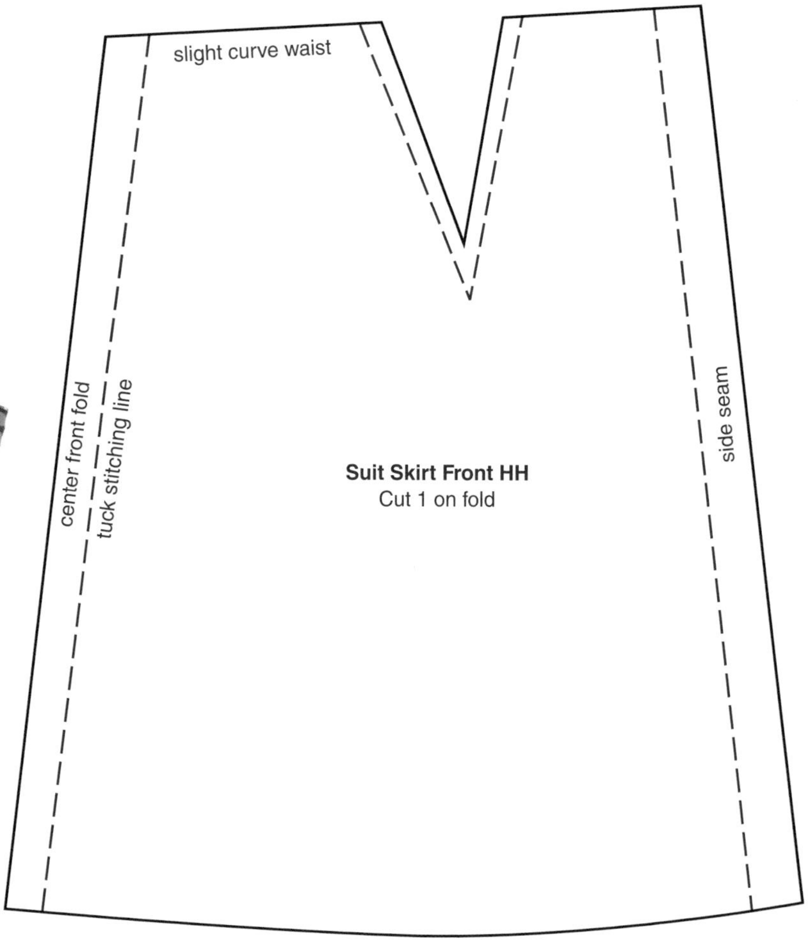

slight curve waist

center front fold

tuck stitching line

side seam

Suit Skirt Front HH
Cut 1 on fold

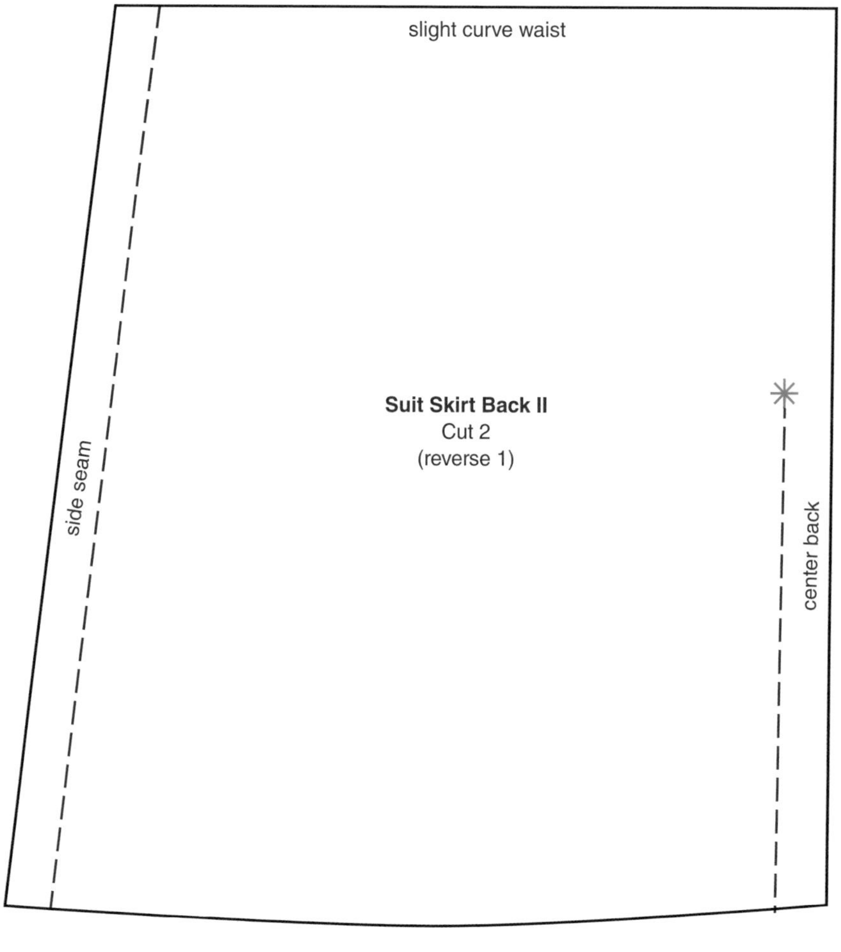

slight curve waist

side seam

Suit Skirt Back II
Cut 2
(reverse 1)

center back

Dressing Up 18" Dolly

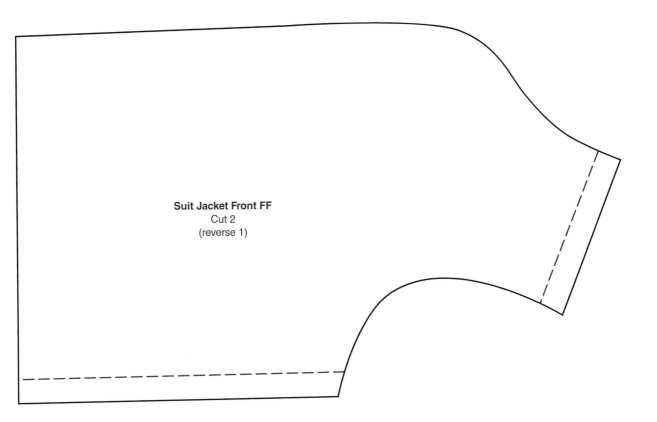

Suit Jacket Front FF
Cut 2
(reverse 1)

Cropped Jacket & Gathered Pants
Instructions on page 24

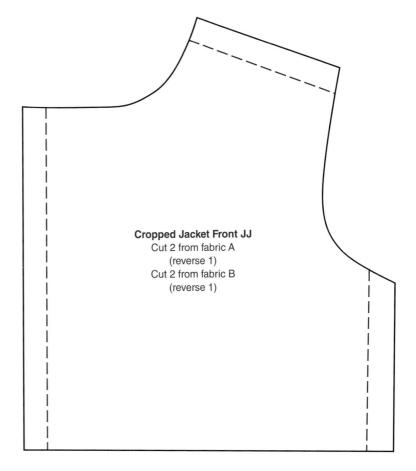

Cropped Jacket Front JJ
Cut 2 from fabric A
(reverse 1)
Cut 2 from fabric B
(reverse 1)

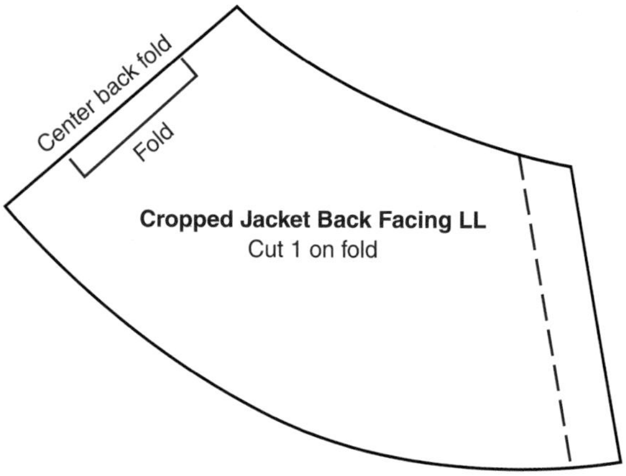

54

Center back fold

Fold

Cropped Jacket Back Facing LL
Cut 1 on fold

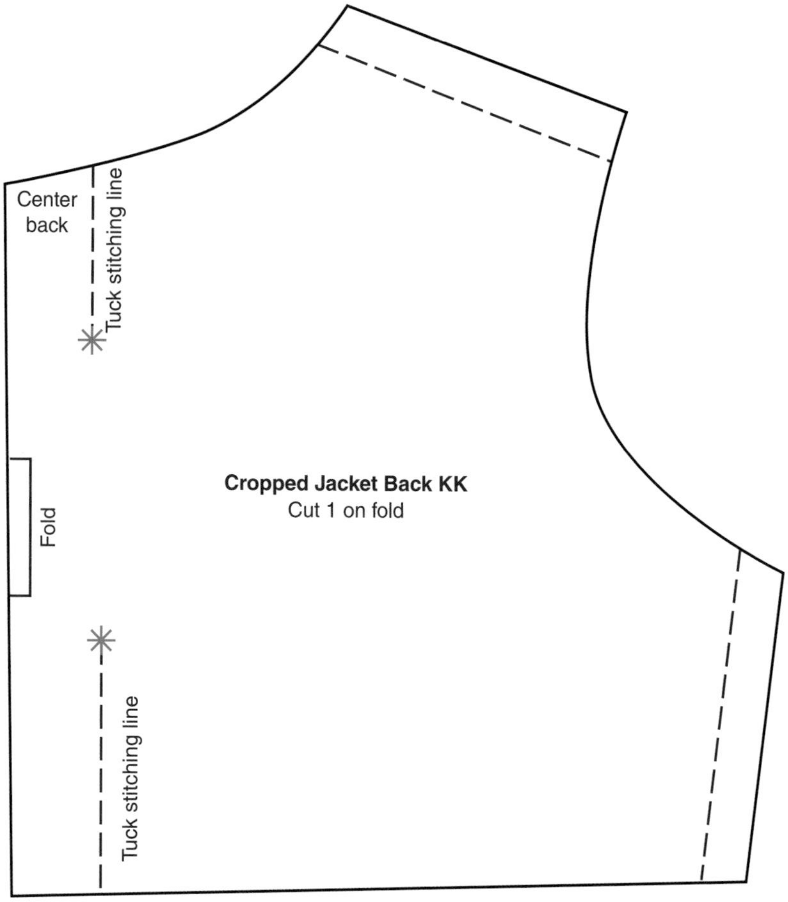

Center
back

Tuck stitching line

Fold

Cropped Jacket Back KK
Cut 1 on fold

Tuck stitching line

side seam

casing line

Gathered Pants Front Upper Leg MM
Cut 2
(reverse 1)

center front seam

inner leg seam

Dressing Up 18" Dolly

Gathered Pants Lower Leg Front NN
Cut 2
(reverse 1)

inner leg seam

side seam

gathering lines

Shirtdress
Instructions on page 28

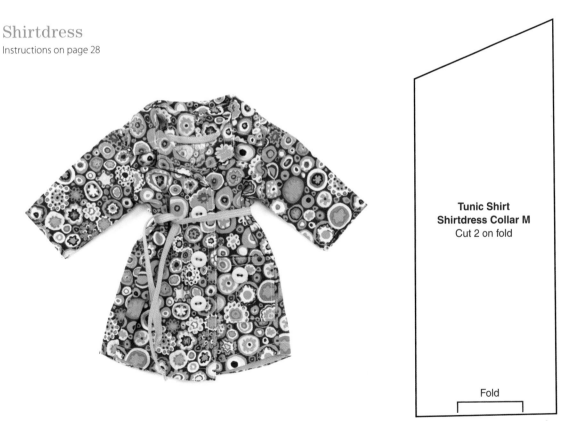

Tunic Shirt
Shirtdress Collar M
Cut 2 on fold

Fold

House of White Birches, Berne, Indiana 46711   Clotilde.com

Color Blocked A-Line Dress
Instructions on page 31

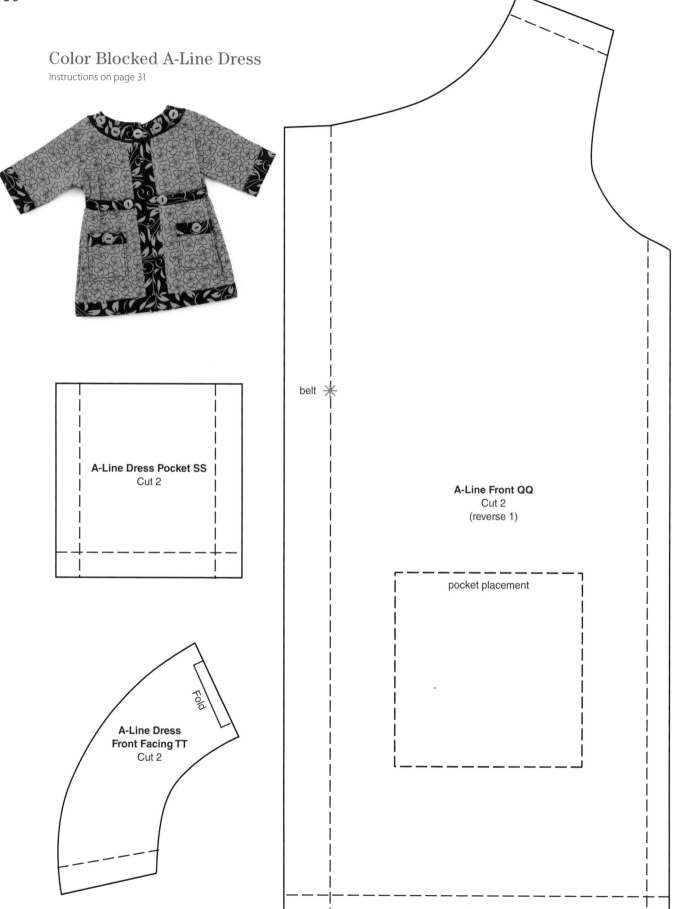

A-Line Dress Pocket SS
Cut 2

**A-Line Dress
Front Facing TT**
Cut 2

Fold

belt ✳

A-Line Front QQ
Cut 2
(reverse 1)

pocket placement

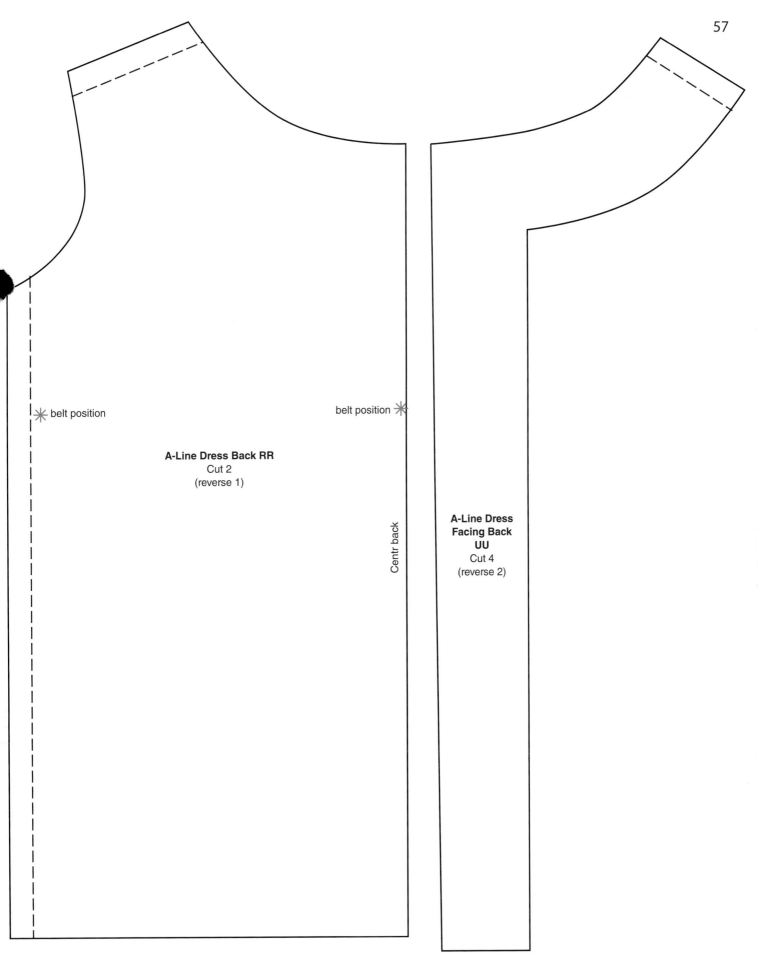

✳ belt position

belt position ✳

A-Line Dress Back RR
Cut 2
(reverse 1)

Centr back

**A-Line Dress
Facing Back
UU**
Cut 4
(reverse 2)

House of White Birches, Berne, Indiana 46711   Clotilde.com

Wool Dress Coat
Instructions on page 33

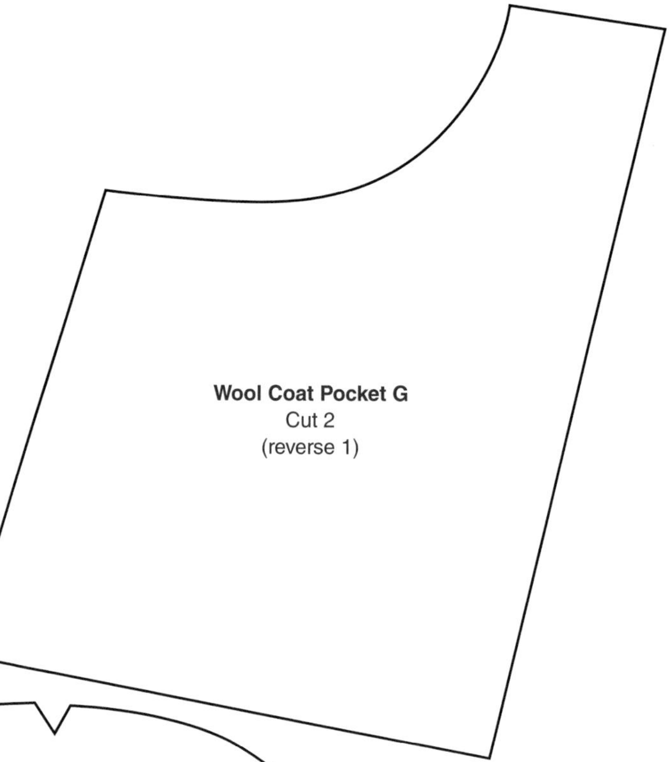

Wool Coat Pocket G
Cut 2
(reverse 1)

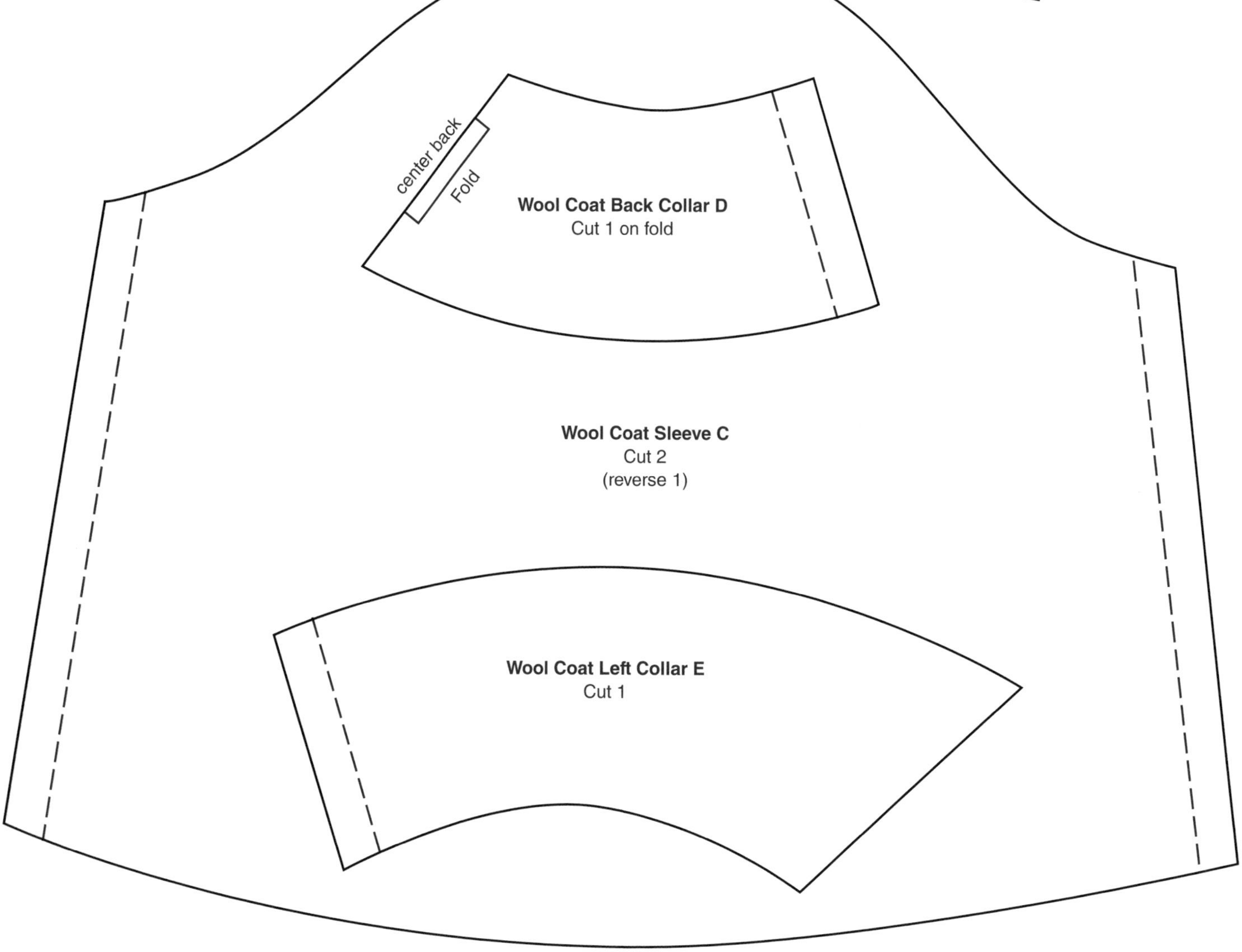

center back

Fold

Wool Coat Back Collar D
Cut 1 on fold

Wool Coat Sleeve C
Cut 2
(reverse 1)

Wool Coat Left Collar E
Cut 1

Wool Coat Right Collar F
Cut 1

Wool Coat Front A
Cut 2
(reverse 1)

pocket placement

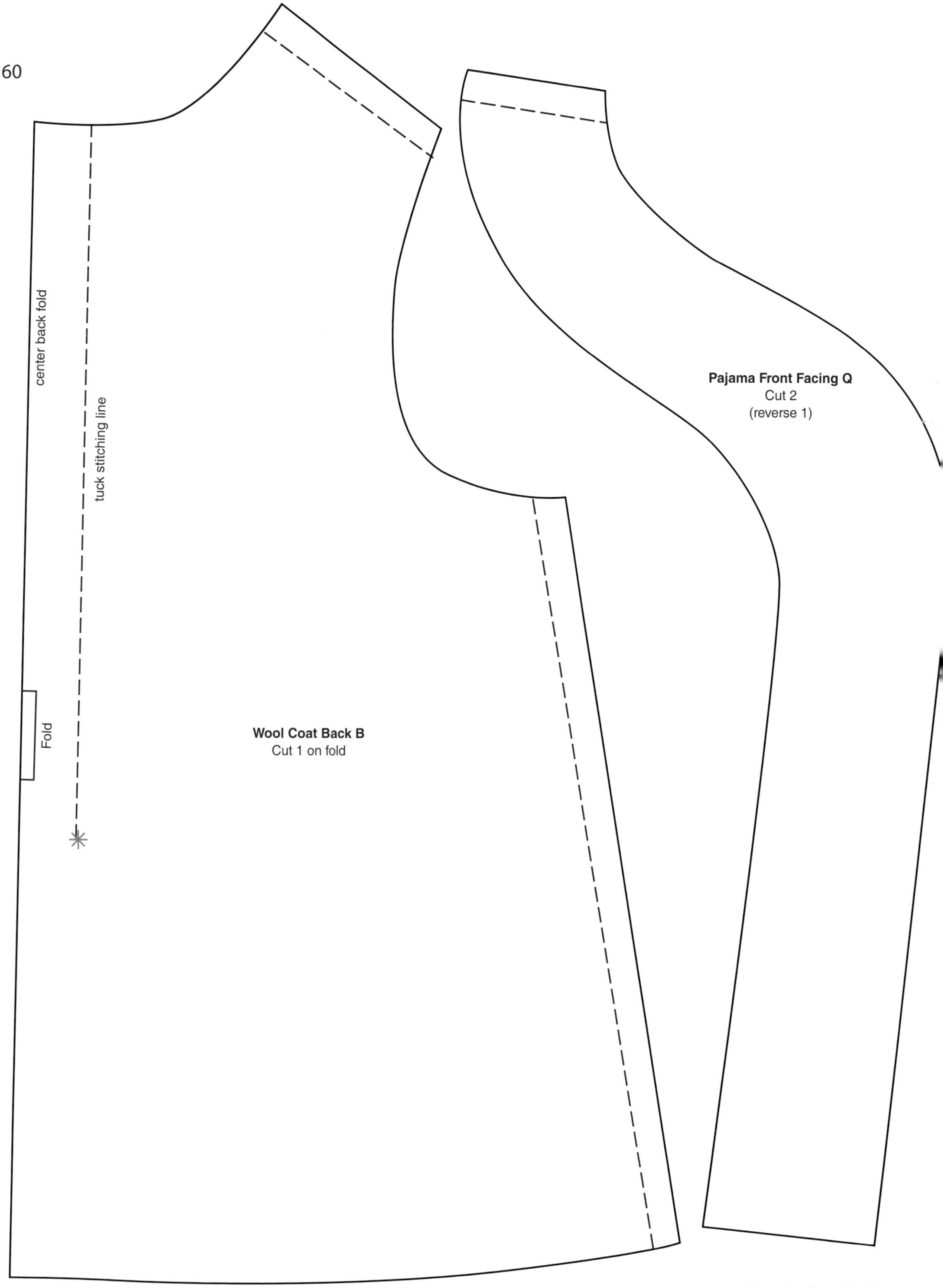

center back fold

tuck stitching line

Fold

Wool Coat Back B
Cut 1 on fold

Pajama Front Facing Q
Cut 2
(reverse 1)

Asian-Inspired Pajamas
Instructions on page 36

center back fold

Fold

Pajama Back P
Cut 1 on fold

**Pajama Top
Back Facing R**
Cut 1 on fold

Fold

center back fold

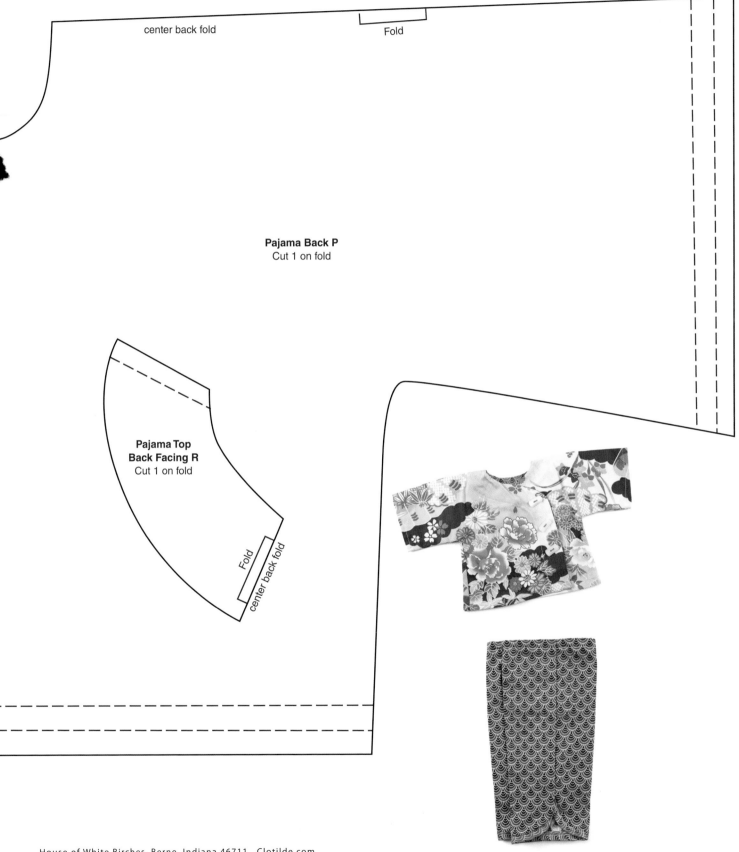

House of White Birches, Berne, Indiana 46711   Clotilde.com

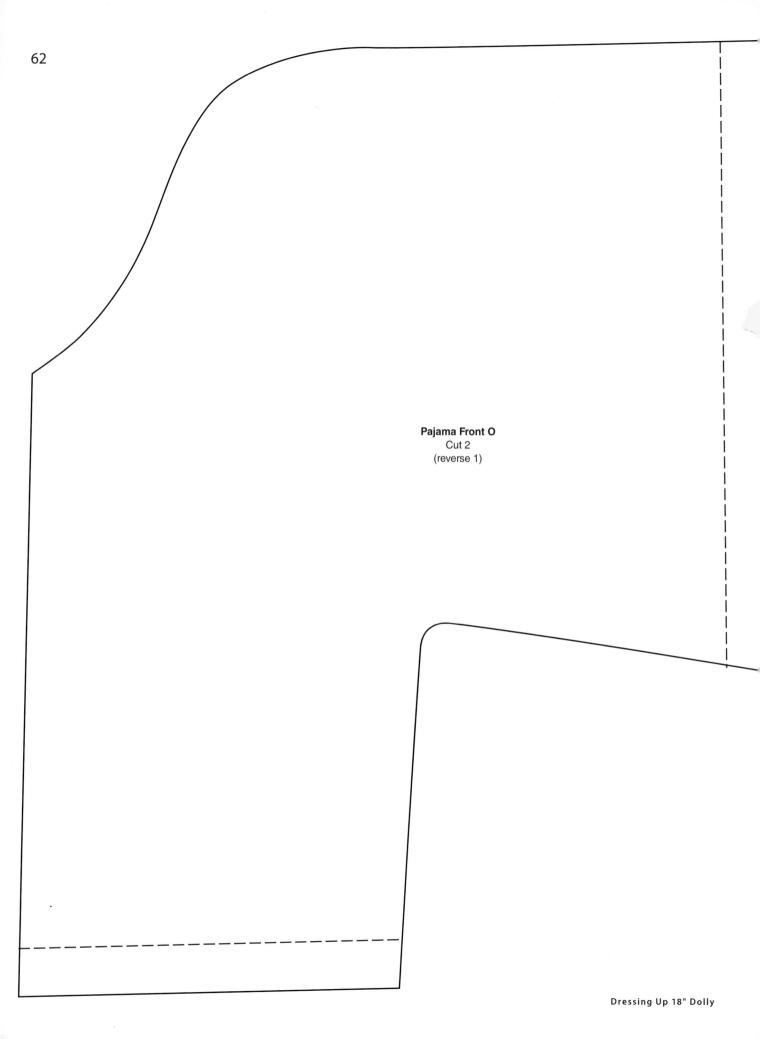

Pajama Front O
Cut 2
(reverse 1)

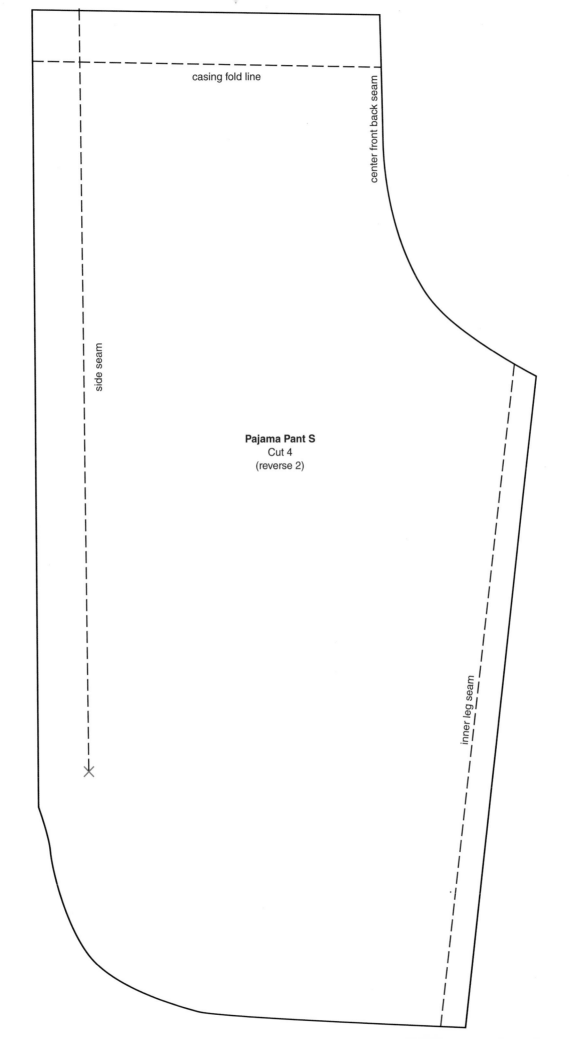

casing fold line

center front back seam

side seam

Pajama Pant S
Cut 4
(reverse 2)

inner leg seam

Metric Conversion Charts

Metric Conversions

Canada/U.S. Measurement		Multiplied by	Metric Measurement
yards	x	.9144	= metres (m)
yards	x	91.44	= centimetres (cm)
inches	x	2.54	= centimetres (cm)
inches	x	25.40	= millimetres (mm)
inches	x	.0254	= metres (m)

Canada/U.S. Measurement		Multiplied by	Metric Measurement
centimetres	x	.3937	= inches
metres	x	1.0936	= yards

Standard Equivalents

Canada/U.S. Measurement		Metric Measurement		Metric Measurement
⅛ inch	=	3.20 mm	=	0.32 cm
¼ inch	=	6.35 mm	=	0.635 cm
⅜ inch	=	9.50 mm	=	0.95 cm
½ inch	=	12.70 mm	=	1.27 cm
⅝ inch	=	15.90 mm	=	1.59 cm
¾ inch	=	19.10 mm	=	1.91 cm
⅞ inch	=	22.20 mm	=	2.22 cm
1 inch	=	25.40 mm	=	2.54 cm
⅛ yard	=	11.43 cm	=	0.11 m
¼ yard	=	22.86 cm	=	0.23 m
⅜ yard	=	34.29 cm	=	0.34 m
½ yard	=	45.72 cm	=	0.46 m
⅝ yard	=	57.15 cm	=	0.57 m
¾ yard	=	68.58 cm	=	0.69 m
⅞ yard	=	80.00 cm	=	0.80 m
1 yard	=	91.44 cm	=	0.91 m
1⅛ yards	=	102.87 cm	=	1.03 m
1¼ yards	=	114.30 cm	=	1.14 m
1⅜ yards	=	125.73 cm	=	1.26 m
1½ yards	=	137.16 cm	=	1.37 m
1⅝ yards	=	148.59 cm	=	1.49 m
1¾ yards	=	160.02 cm	=	1.60 m
1⅞ yards	=	171.44 cm	=	1.71 m
2 yards	=	182.88 cm	=	1.83 m
2⅛ yards	=	194.31 cm	=	1.94 m
2¼ yards	=	205.74 cm	=	2.06 m
2⅜ yards	=	217.17 cm	=	2.17 m
2½ yards	=	228.60 cm	=	2.29 m
2⅝ yards	=	240.03 cm	=	2.40 m
2¾ yards	=	251.46 cm	=	2.51 m
2⅞ yards	=	262.88 cm	=	2.63 m
3 yards	=	274.32 cm	=	2.74 m
3⅛ yards	=	285.75 cm	=	2.86 m
3¼ yards	=	297.18 cm	=	2.97 m
3⅜ yards	=	308.61 cm	=	3.09 m
3½ yards	=	320.04 cm	=	3.20 m
3⅝ yards	=	331.47 cm	=	3.31 m
3¾ yards	=	342.90 cm	=	3.43 m
3⅞ yards	=	354.32 cm	=	3.54 m
4 yards	=	365.76 cm	=	3.66 m
4⅛ yards	=	377.19 cm	=	3.77 m
4¼ yards	=	388.62 cm	=	3.89 m
4⅜ yards	=	400.05 cm	=	4.00 m
4½ yards	=	411.48 cm	=	4.11 m
4⅝ yards	=	422.91 cm	=	4.23 m
4¾ yards	=	434.34 cm	=	4.34 m
4⅞ yards	=	445.76 cm	=	4.46 m
5 yards	=	457.20 cm	=	4.57 m

HOUSE of WHITE BIRCHES PUBLISHERS SINCE 1947

Dressing Up 18" Dolly is published by DRG, 306 East Parr Road, Berne, IN 46711. Printed in USA. Copyright © 2010 DRG. All rights reserved. This publication may not be reproduced in part or in whole without written permission from the publisher.

RETAIL STORES: If you would like to carry this pattern book or any other DRG publications, visit DRGwholesale.com

Every effort has been made to ensure that the instructions in this pattern book are complete and accurate. We cannot, however, take responsibility for human error, typographical mistakes or variations in individual work. Please visit ClotildeCustomerCare.com to check for pattern updates.

ISBN: 978-1-59217-312-9
1 2 3 4 5 6 7 8 9